TABLE OF CONTENTS

INTRODUCTION P.2

■ **FINDINGS** P.5

■ **RANKINGS** P.9
- Top 100 modern art
- Top 100 contemporary art
- Top 5 lots sold at auction all categories
- Top 10 modern art lots sold at auction
- Top 10 contemporary art lots sold at auction

■ **MARKETPLACES** P.21

■ **AUCTION HOUSE MARKET SHARE** P.31

■ **THE DIASPORA** P.35
AND THE GLOBAL ART DISCOURSE
- Overview by Osei G. Kofi
- Julia Grosse & Yvette Mutumba
- Tumelo Mosaka
- Mimi Errol
- Mustapha Orif
- Lionel Manga
- Nii Andrews

■ **ARTISTS IN THE DIASPORA** P.53
- Wanguechi Mutu
- Yinka Shonibare

■ **2016 TEACH THE FUTURE** P.59
- Makgati Molebatsi
- Moncef Msakni
- Julia Grosse & Yvette Mutumba
- Tumelo Mosaka
- Mustapha Orif

INTRODUCTION

THE SEGMENT THAT RESISTS THE ART MARKET CRISIS

The global market of modern and contemporary African art performed strongly in 2016 with a sell-through rate of 72% in a morose context of the international art market and the slowing-down of African economies. This segment proved to be an exception.

This vitality was led by modern art[1] with a sell-through rate of 76% and 55% in value of the total amount of sales, reaching US$23.3 million. Contemporary art[2], the majority of acquired works being by artists appearing at auction for the first time, had a sell-through rate of 66%.
The works sold beyond their high estimates represented 58% in value of the total number of sales during the year, including 66.9% for modern art and 33% for contemporary art.

Bids that exceeded the symbolic threshold of US$1 million rose by 200%, including 50% for modern art and 50% for contemporary art. Among the buoyant examples was the extremely mediatised Bowie/Collector sale organised by Sotheby's in London on 10-11 November 2016 saw all 17 works by African artists find buyers, the works totalling £341,875 (with buyer premium), equivalent to US$425,504 seven times over the pre-sale estimate.

Arthouse Contemporary, the Nigerian auction house in Lagos, went from having two annual sales in 2015 to three in 2016.

There are several reasons for these results, the first being the strong potential in artistic and market value of the works proposed in galleries and at auctions. Secondly, the huge direct and indirect investments, such as institutional, commercial and non-commercial projects and exhibitions, mainly in western countries as well as new structural initiatives in Africa. The buyer base has also increased. Furthermore, reference prices have recently been consolidated: the average range of estimates of works proposed for auction were between US$7,140 and US$9,650 for modernist works and between US$7,420 and US$10,260 for contemporary art. This represents a progression of 60% and 70% respectively over seven years.

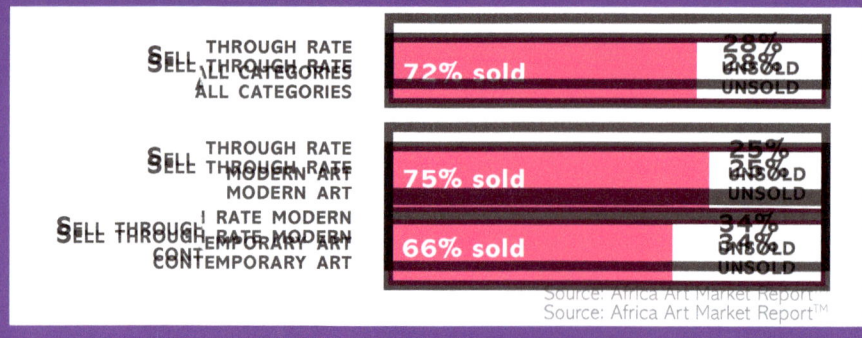

SELL THROUGH RATE ALL CATEGORIES — 72% sold / 28% UNSOLD
SELL THROUGH RATE MODERN ART — 75% sold / 25% UNSOLD
SELL THROUGH RATE CONTEMPORARY ART — 66% sold / 34% UNSOLD

Source: Africa Art Market Report™

1- Artists whose birth range from 1850 through 1939
2- Artists who were born after 1940

We are witnessing the first effects of the current structural changes that were observed in our previous reports. This market is at the end of a long cycle that could be defined as being "rudimentary" and right at the start of a new modernity. The trend is growing and its rhythm will be defined by how actors on the African continent organise themselves by becoming meaningfully and clearly involved in the economy and art market, how actors in classical African arts (African statuaries and masks) control their market, and the savoir-faire by the new generation of actors involved in this segment.

Strauss & Co, based in Johannesburg, South Africa, is the leading auction house for the total amount of works sold with 31% in value and 57% of lots.

London held the most important place in the market in 2016, considering the number of operators in our study that organised sales (40% of the total), the number of proposed lots (2.9% of the total) and of sold lots (28.1% and US$11.9 million in the year) and institutional and commercial exhibitions. We'll see how this pans out during the post-Brexit period.

Three factors can explain the attractiveness of the British capital for modern and contemporary African art: its number one place in finance; its appeal to African creators and investors, mainly from South Africa, Nigeria and Ghana; and the established and prosperous African diaspora involved in artistic/cultural initiatives and institutions, such as the Tate.

For players based on the African continent, the evolution of the sector is dazzling. But it is not felt in the same way by those from western countries due to differences in expectations and costs. At public sales in Africa, Europe and the US, records have become commonplace and galleries on the three continents remain in the same dynamic.

One of the pillars of this segment's improvement is the African diaspora. In this new report, we have decided to scrutinize its contribution, importance and impact because for a long time it has been active in making African art the segment with the biggest growth potential in the art market.

HOW TO BE PART OF THE AFRICAN ART BOOM

Appraisal & valuation of your artwork by our expert within 48 hours
and/or sell it on the best price

.

FREE OF CHARGE

.

contact@africartmarket.today

Fill the easy inqury form here www.africartmarket.today

Findings

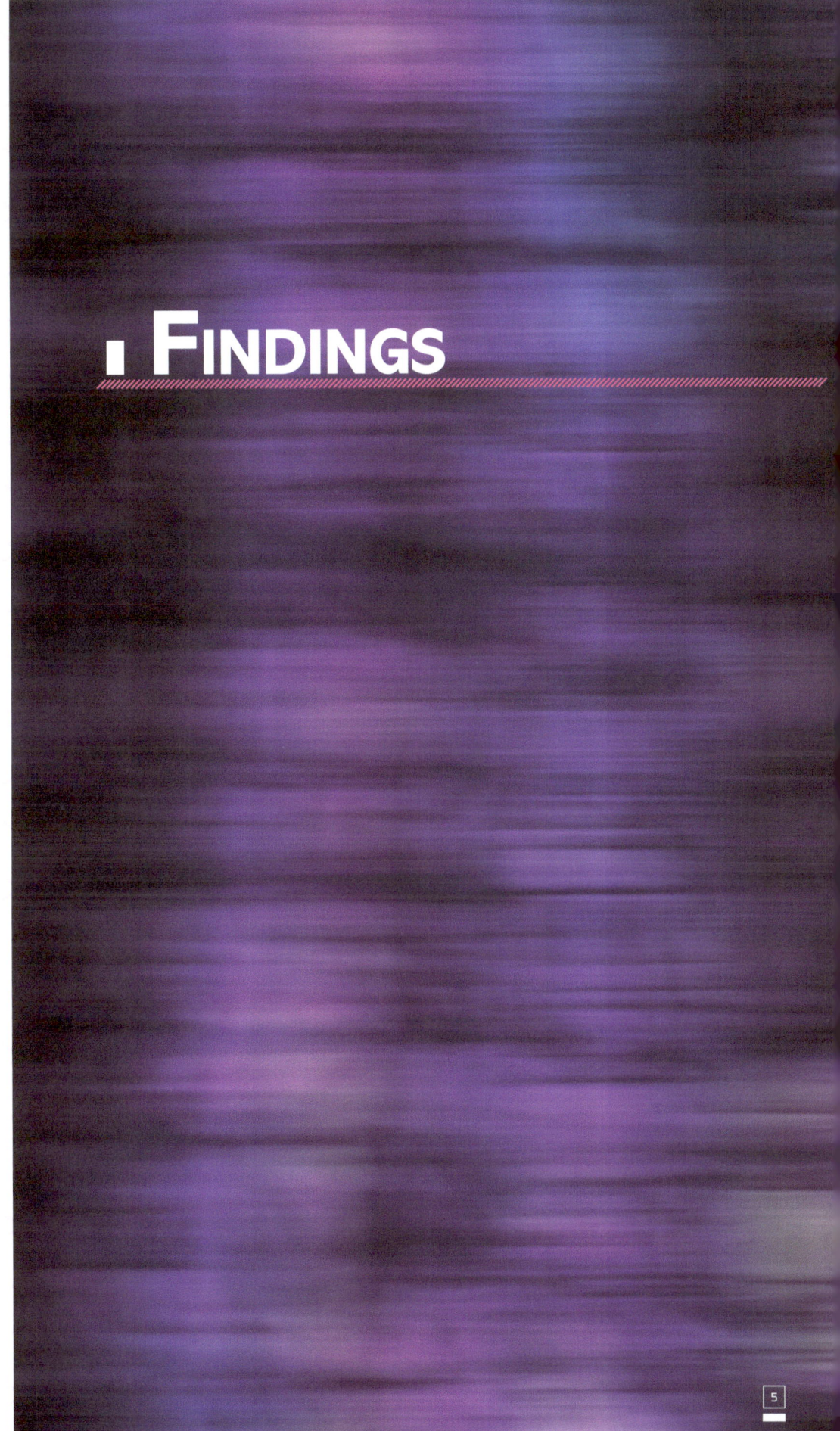

This segment, which had a sell-through rate of 72%, proved to be an exception to the morose context of the international art market and the slowing-down of African economies in 2016.

Bids that exceeded the symbolic threshold of US$1 million rose by 200%, including 50% for modern art and 50% for contemporary art.

Strauss & Co, based in Johannesburg, South Africa, is the leading auction house for the total amount of works sold with 31% in value and 57% of lots.

Modern art led the market with a sell-through rate of 76%, and 55% in value of the total amount of sales, reaching US$23.3 million.

London held the most important place in the market in 2016, considering the number of operators in our study that organised sales (40% of the total), the number of proposed lots (2.9% of the total) and of sold lots (28.1% and US$11.9 million in the year) and institutional and commercial exhibitions.

The enlargement of the buyers' base in all categories.

In contemporary art, the works sold beyond their high estimates, representing 58% in value, or US$8 million, and 37.9% between their estimates or US$5,7 million with regard to the total number of sales in this category.

Female artists continue to lead this market for the second consecutive year and constitute a very important market share. They represent 60% of the top five most expensive selling lots in all categories and 66.5% in value for this same ranking.

Despite the majority of auction houses being young, they recorded a strong dynamic and good results, sales organised on the African continent counting for 46.1% of the total value, fetching US$19.6 million and 93.2% of lots.

The most expensive work sold in any category is South African-born artist Marlene Dumas's painting, "Night nurse" (1999-2000), which sold for US$2.5 million at Phillips New-York in 2016.

Lawrence Lemaoana (b.1982)
Real Power is not granted it is
performed, 2017 - Khanga textile and cotton
embroidery, 155x115 cm, court. Afronova

RANKINGS

Methodology

- Top 100 modern art
- Top 100 contemporary art
- Top 5 lots sold at auction all categories
- Top 10 modern art lots sold at auction
- Top 10 contemporary art lots sold at auction

METHODOLOGY MODERN ART

Given the specifics of the burgeoning African modern art market, it is essential to go beyond auction results alone in order to analyze it. This study ranks the 100 artists- whose birth range from 1850 through 1939 -who obtained the best scores according to four weighted criteria:

1. turnover at auction in 2016[1] (40%)
2. medium price of characteristic artworks on the first market (10%)
3. number of exhibitions in museums throughout career (25%)
4. number of exhibitions at commercial galleries throughout career (25%)

3 ARTIST PROFILES

3 different artist profiles emerged through the analysis:

Global
The Global profile includes artists who are recognized internationally in both the museum and the commercial worlds, with stable prices on the first and the second markets.

Undervalued
The Undervalued profile includes artists with a strong presence on the art scene, both in the non-profit and the first market sectors.
Their artworks appear sporadically on the second market, with undervalued prices.

High Potential
The High Potential profile includes artists whose recognition in the art circles is underway. Their presence is stronger in museums than in commercial galleries. Their artworks are hardly seen on the second market.

1- Based on auction results from Bonhams, Christies, Phillips, Sotheby's, Art House, CMOOA, Cornette de St Cyr, Piasa and Strauss & Co. between January and December 2016 excluding buyer's premium.

TOP 100 MODERN

N°	ARTIST	COUNTRY OF ORIGIN	DATES	Painting	Drawing	Collage	Print	Sculpture	Installation	Photography	Video Performance	Performance	CATEGORY	TOTAL SALES 2016 (USD)	SCORE
1	Irma Stern	South Africa	1894-1966	•									Global Modern	3 269 920	7.94
2	Omar El Nagdi	Egypt	1931-1975	•									Global Modern	954 167	5.59
3	Alexis Preller	South Africa	1911-1994	•									Global Modern	1 726 098	5.51
4	Ben Enwonwu	Nigeria	1917-1994	•									Global Modern	1 062 655	5.50
5	Walter Battiss	South Africa	1906-1982	•			•	•					Global Modern	901 641	5.23
6	Farid Belkahia	Morocco	1934-2014	•									Global Modern	560 526	5.15
7	Mahmoud Said	Egypt	1897-1964	•									Global Modern	817 613	5.07
8	Robert Griffiths Hodgins	South Africa	1920-2010	•			•	•					Global Modern	906 412	4.93
9	Jacob Hendrik Pierneef	South Africa	1886-1957	•									Global Modern	880 033	4.90
10	Malick Sidibé	Mali	1936-2016							•			Global Modern	10 808	4.76
11	Mahmoud Mokhtar	Egypt	1891-1934					•					Global Modern	558 098	4.50
12	Hamed Ewais	Egypt	1919-2011	•				•					Global Modern	504 167	4.43
13	Erik Laubscher	South Africa	1927-2013	•									Global Modern	213 904	4.37
14	Ablade Glover	Ghana	1934	•									Global Modern	94 186	4.32
15	Ibrahim El-Salahi	Sudan	1930	•									Undervalued Modern	32 012	4.29
16	Gregoire Johannes Boonzaier	South Africa	1909-2005	•			•						Global Modern	326 814	4.26
17	Peter Clarke	South Africa	1929-2014		•		•						Global Modern	272 594	4.19
18	Jilali Gharbaoui	Morocco	1930-1971	•	•								Global Modern	87 380	4.06
19	Christo Coetzee	South Africa	1929-2000	•									Global Modern	150 929	4.04
20	David Goldblatt	South Africa	1930							•			Undervalued Modern	3 670	4.00
21	Esther Mahlangu	South Africa	1935	•				•					High Potential	1 422	4.00
22	Mohamed Chebaa	Morocco	1935-2013	•									Global Modern	103 220	3.98
23	Yusuf Adebayo Grillo	Nigeria	1934	•									Global Modern	556 514	3.90
24	Seydou Keita	Mali	1921-2001							•			Global Modern	0	3.85
25	Hussein Bikar	Egypt	1912-2002	•									Global Modern	189 446	3.84
26	Vladimir Grigoryevich Tretchikoff	South Africa	1913-2006	•									Global Modern	505 528	3.83
27	Pranas Domsaitis	South Africa	1880-1965	•									Global Modern	73 615	3.82
28	Samir Rafi	Egypt	1926-2004	•									Undervalued Modern	50 000	3.81
29	Ahmed Cherkaoui	Morocco	1934-1967	•									Global Modern	155 608	3.79
30	Anton van Wouw	South Africa	1862-1945	•									Global Modern	152 759	3.79
31	Cecil Edwin Frans Skotnes	South Africa	1926-2009	•									Global Modern	408 735	3.76
32	Maurice Charles Louis Van Essche	South Africa	1906-1977	•									Global Modern	94 166	3.74
33	Pieter Hugo Naudé	South Africa	1869-1941	•									Global Modern	191 675	3.71
34	Saad Ben Cheffaj	Morocco	1939	•									High Potential	66 903	3.68

Source: Africa Art Market Report™

TOP 100 MODERN

N°	ARTIST	COUNTRY OF ORIGIN	DATES	Painting	Drawing	Collage	Print	Sculpture	Installation	Photography	Video	Performance	CATEGORY	TOTAL SALES 2016 (USD)	SCORE
35	Stanley Faraday Pinker	South Africa	1924-2012	•									Global Modern	250 221	3,66
36	Frans Martin Claerhout	South Africa	1919-2006	•									Global Modern	48 341	3,66
37	Edoardo Daniele Villa	South Africa	1915-2011	•									Global Modern	130 842	3,61
38	François Krige	South Africa	1913-1994	•	•								Global Modern	88 912	3,61
39	Adriaan Hendrik Boshoff	South Africa	1935-2007	•									Global Modern	204 151	3,61
40	Mohammed Melehi	Morocco	1936	•									Global Modern	177 382	3,57
41	Abdul Hadi El Gazzar	Egypt	1925-1965	•	•								Global Modern	174 167	3,57
42	Mahmoud Moussa	Egypt	1913-2003					•					Undervalued Modern	42 000	3,55
43	Mohammad Naghi	Egypt	1888-1956	•									Undervalued Modern	31 907	3,54
44	Ahmed Ben Driss El Yacoubi	Morocco	1928-1985	•									Global Modern	145 533	3,53
45	Fatma Haddad Baya	Algeria	1931-1998	•									Undervalued Modern	3 682	3,50
46	Alexander Rose-Innes	South Africa	1915-1996	•									Global Modern	73 612	3,44
47	Chaïbia Tallal	Morocco	1929-2004	•									Global Modern	68 716	3,44
48	Errol Stephen Boyley	South Africa	1918-2007	•									Global Modern	66 278	3,43
49	Gladys Mgludlandlu	South Africa	1917-1979	•	•								Undervalued	18 579	3,42
50	Gerard Sekoto	South Africa	1913-1993	•									Global Modern	178 194	3,42
51	Ephraim Mojalefa Ngatane	South Africa	1938-1971	•									Undervalued Modern	57 625	3,42
52	Maud Frances Eyston Sumner	South Africa	1902-1985	•									Global Modern	173 110	3,42
53	J.D. Okhai Ojeikere	Nigeria	1930-2014							•			Undervalued Modern	0	3,40
54	Lucas Tandokwazi Sithole	South Africa	1931-1994					•					Global Modern	66 693	3,33
55	Andrew Clement Verster	South Africa	1937	•									Global Modern	61 439	3,33
56	Adolph Stephan Friedrich Jentsch	Namibia	1888-1977	•									Global Modern	59 231	3,32
57	Alfred Neville Lewis	South Africa	1895-1972	•									Global Modern	41 953	3,30
58	Bruce Onobrakpeya	Nigeria	1932				•	•					Undervalued Modern	21 457	3,28
59	Effat Naghi	Egypt	1905-1994	•									High Potential	12 272	3,27
60	Pieter Willem Frederick Wenning	South Africa	1873-1921	•									Global Modern	69 421	3,19
61	David Nthubu Koloane	South Africa	1938	•									High Potential	26 167	3,18
62	Robert Gwelo Goodman	South Africa	1871-1939	•									Undervalued Modern	65 318	3,18
63	Frans David Oerder	South Africa	1867-1944	•									Global Modern	60 469	3,18
64	Uche Okeke	Nigeria	1933-2016	•	•								High Potential	17 505	3,17
65	Amos Langdown	South Africa	1930-2006	•									Undervalued Modern	15 703	3,17
66	Alexander "Skunder" Boghossian	Ethiopia	1937-2003	•									Undervalued Modern	14 535	3,17
67	Ezrom Legae	South Africa	1938-1999			•		•					High Potential	3 592	3,15
68	Georges Lilanga	Tanzania	1934-2005					•					Global Modern	1 656	3,15

Source: Africa Art Market Report™

TOP 100 MODERN

N°	ARTIST	COUNTRY OF ORIGIN	DATES	Painting	Drawing	Collage	Print	Sculpture	Installation	Photography	Video	Performance	CATEGORY	TOTAL SALES 2016 (USD)	SCORE
69	Maggie Laubser	South Africa	1886-1973	•			•						Global Modern	346 465	3,13
70	Inji Efflatoun	Egypt	1924-1989	•									Global Modern	17 000	3,12
71	Freida Lock	South Africa	1902-1962	•									Global Modern	79 118	3,10
72	Hassan El Glaoui	Morocco	1923	•									High Potential	65 960	3,08
73	Terence John Mccaw	South Africa	1913-1978	•									Global Modern	58 325	3,07
74	George Milwa Mnyaluza Pemba	South Africa	1912-2001	•									Global Modern	56 635	3,07
75	Tinus (Marthinus Johannes) De Jongh	South Africa	1885-1942	•									Global Modern	56 277	3,07
76	Jan Ernst Abraham Volschenk	South Africa	1853-1936	•									Undervalued Modern	55 237	3,07
77	Gerard de Leeuw	South Africa	1912-1985					•					High Potential	49 163	3,06
78	Wolf Kibel	South Africa	1903-1938	•			•						Global Modern	24 724	3,03
79	Johannes Segogela	South Africa	1936					•					Undervalusted Modern	2 292	3,00
80	Abdallah Benanteur	Algeria	1931	•									High Potential	0	3,00
81	Jak Katarikawe	Uganda	1940	•									High Potential	0	3,00
82	Harry Stratford Caldecott	South Africa	1886-1929	•									Global Modern	91 894	2,96
83	Conrad Nagel Doman Theys	South Africa	1940	•									Global Modern	35 478	2,94
84	Eleanor Frances Esmonde-White	South Africa	1914-2007	•									Undervalued Modern	35 018	2,94
85	Cecily Sash	South Africa	1925				•						High Potential	34 699	2,94
86	Titta Fasciotti	South Africa	1927-1993	•									Global Modern	30 728	2,94
87	Demas Nwoko	Nigeria	1935	•									Undervalued Modern	26 191	2,93
88	Bettie Cilliers-Barnard	South Africa	1914-2010	•									Undervalued Modern	25 813	2,93
89	Simon Okeke	Nigeria	1937-1969	•									Undervalued Modern	14 551	2,92
90	Susanne Wenger	Nigeria	1915-2009	•			•						High Potential	0	2,90
91	Larry (Laurence Vincent) Scully	South Africa	1922-2002	•									High Potential	37 936	2,80
92	Amon Kotei	Ghana	1915-2011	•									Undervalued Modern	20 000	2,77
93	Sydney Alex Kumalo	South Africa	1935-1988					•					Global Modern	131 866	2,76
94	Ousmane Sow	Senegal	1935-2016					•					High Potential	0	2,75
95	Dorothy Moss Kay	South Africa	1886-1964	•									Undervalued Modern	35 791	2,69
96	Afewerk Tekle	Ethiopia	1932-2012	•									High Potential	8 730	2,66
97	Stella Shawzin	South Africa	1929					•					Undervalued	6 399	2,66
98	Johannes Petrus Meintjes	South Africa	1923-1980	•									Undervalued Modern	103	2,65
99	Ngwenya Valente Malangatana	Mozambique	1936-2011	•									Undervalued modern	20 579	2,53
100	Ernest Mancoba	South Africa	1904-2002	•									Global Modern	0	2,40

Source: Africa Art Market Report™

METHODOLOGY CONTEMPORARY ART

Given the specifics of the burgeoning contemporary art market, it is essential to go beyond auction results alone in order to analyze it. This study ranks the 100 artists —who were born after 1940— who obtained the best scores according to five weighted criteria:

1. turnover at auction in 2016[1] (25%)
2. medium price of characteristic artworks on the first market (25%)
3. number of exhibitions in museums throughout career (20%)
4. number of exhibitions at commercial galleries throughout career (20%)
5. level of recognition among independent art critics (10%)

4 ARTIST PROFILES

4 different artist profiles emerged through the analysis:

Global
The Global profile includes artists who are recognized internationally in both the museum and the commercial worlds, with stable prices on the first and the second markets.

Undervalued
The Undervalued profile includes artists with a strong presence on the art scene, both in the non-profit and the first market sectors. Their artworks appear sporadically on the second market, with undervalued prices.

High Potential
The High Potential profile includes artists whose recognition in the art circles is underway. Their presence is stronger in museums than in commercial galleries. Their artworks are hardly seen on the second market.

To watch
The To Watch profile includes emerging artists whose first artworks have recently been seen on the second market for the first time.

---

1 - Based on auction results from Bonhams, Christies, Phillips, Sotheby's, Art House, CMOOA, Cornette de St Cyr, Piasa and Strauss & Co. between January and December 2016 excluding buyer's premium.

TOP 100 CONTEMPORY

N°	ARTIST	COUNTRY OF ORIGIN	DATES	Painting	Drawing	Collage	Print	Sculpture	Installation	Photography	Video	Performance	CATEGORY	TOTAL SALES 2016 (USD)	SCORE
1	Marlene Dumas	South Africa	1953	•									Global Contemporary	3 205 284	7,45
2	William Kentridge	South Africa	1955	•	•	•	•		•				Global Contemporary	764 008	6,56
3	Julie Mehretu	Ethiopia	1970	•									Global Contemporary	1 372 748	6,27
4	Yinka Shonibare	Nigeria	1962					•					Global Contemporary	100 584	6,03
5	Ibrahim El Anatsui	Ghana	1944					•	•				Global Contemporary	1 154 565	6,00
6	Wangechi Mutu	Kenya	1972	•	•			•					Global Contemporary	279 117	5,65
7	Candice Breitz	South Africa	1972						•	•	•		Global Contemporary	13 527	5,55
8	Kendell Geers	South Africa	1968					•	•	•		•	High Potential	14 113	5,45
9	Njideka Akunyili Crosby	Nigeria	1983	•	•								Global Contemporary	985 417	5,39
10	Pascale Marthine Tayou	Cameroon	1967										Global Contemporary	0	5,35
11	Pieter Hugo	South Africa	1976							•			High Potential	9 271	5,25
12	Ibrahim Mahama	Ghana	1983					•	•				To Watch	0	5,25
13	Romuald Hazoume	Benin	1962	•				•	•				Global Contemporary	90 928	5,23
14	Robin Rhode	South Africa	1976							•	•		Global Contemporary	32 904	5,18
15	Roger Ballen	South Africa	1950							•			High Potential	8 786	5,18
16	John Akomfrah	Ghana	1957								•		Global Contemporary	0	5,18
17	Barthelemy Toguo	Cameroon	1967		•			•	•				Global Contemporary	4 689	5,05
18	Mounir Fatmi	Morocco	1970					•		•			Global Contemporary	69 681	4,92
19	Abdoulaye Konate	Mali	1953					•					Global Contemporary	0	4,85
20	Latifa Echakhch	Morocco	1974	•				•	•				Global Contemporary	51 313	4,82
21	Cheri Samba	Congo	1956	•					•				Global Contemporary	63 330	4,77
22	Lalla Essaydi	Morocco	1956							•			High Potential	20 000	4,76
23	Adel Abdessemed	Algeria	1971		•			•	•			•	Global Contemporary	19 191	4,73
24	Youssef Nabil	Egypt	1972							•			Global Contemporary	0	4,70
25	Diane Victor	South Africa	1964		•	•						•	Global Contemporary	24 128	4,66
26	Lionel Smit	South Africa	1982	•									High Potential	54 658	4,62
27	Kader Attia	Algeria	1970					•	•	•			Global Contemporary	45 000	4,62
28	Soly Cisse	Senegal	1969	•	•						•		High Potential	20 081	4,61
29	Ghada Amer	Egypt	1963	•				•					Global Contemporary	114 877	4,59
30	Otobong Nkanga	Nigeria	1974					•	•				High Potential	0	4,50
31	Aboudia	Ivory Coast	1983	•	•			•					High Potential	78 838	4,48
32	Zwelethu Mthethwa	South Africa	1960							•			High Potential	18 768	4,41
33	Sue (Susan Mary) Williamson	South Africa	1941						•	•			High Potential	8 734	4,40
34	Tracey Rose	South Africa	1974	•					•	•	•	•	High Potential	0	4,40

Source: Africa Art Market Report™

TOP 100 CONTEMPORY

N°	ARTIST	COUNTRY OF ORIGIN	DATES	Painting	Drawing	Collage	Print	Sculpture	Installation	Photography	Video	Performance	CATEGORY	TOTAL SALES 2016 (USD)	SCORE
35	Norman Clive Catherine	South Africa	1949					•					Global Contemporary	299 314	4,35
36	Dumile Feni-Mhlaba	South Africa	1942		•			•					High Potential	3 372	4,35
37	Bodys Izek Kingelez	Congo	1948					•					High Potential	0	4,30
38	Deborah Margaret Bell	South Africa	1957		•		•	•					Global Contemporary	89 479	4,23
39	Jabulane Sam Nhlengethwa	South Africa	1955	•			•	•					High Potential	24 198	4,21
40	Anton Smit	South Africa	1954					•					High Potential	19 652	4,21
41	Zoulikha Bouabdellah	Algeria	1977	•		•	•		•	•	•	•	Undervalued Contemporary	20 904	4,16
42	Moshekwa Langa	South Africa	1975	•	•								To Watch	323	4,15
43	Mahi Binebine	Morocco	1959	•									High Potential	75 966	4,13
44	El Seed	Tunisia	1981	•									To Watch	19 000	4,11
45	Athi-Patra Ruga	South Africa	1984				•		•	•		•	To Watch	8 460	4,10
46	Chiurai Kudzanai	Zimbabwe	1981							•			To Watch	8 056	4,10
47	Mohamed Drissi	Morocco	1946	•	•		•	•					Global Modern	4 357	4,10
48	Cheri Cherin	Congo	1955	•									High Potential	0	4,10
49	Susan Hefuna	Egypt	1962		•			•	•	•	•	•	High Potential	0	4,10
50	Mohammed Kacimi	Morocco	1942-2003	•									Undervalued Contemporary	248 493	4,04
51	Nnenna Okore	Nigeria	1975					•					High Potential	30 987	4,01
52	Samuel Fosso	Cameroon	1962							•			Undervalauted Contemporary	0	4,00
53	Hassan Hajjaj	Morocco	1961					•	•				High Potential	28 469	3,98
54	Monsengwo Kejwamfi "Moke"	Congo	1950	•									High Potential	87 188	3,98
55	Mahjoub Ben Bella	Algeria	1946	•									High Potential	32 022	3,96
56	Twins Seven Seven	Nigeria	1944	•	•		•						High Potential	5 100	3,95
57	Michael Armitage	Kenya	1984	•									High Potential	0	3,95
58	Antonio Ole	Angola	1951	•				•	•				High Potential	28 004	3,91
59	Willie (William) Bester	South Africa	1956							•			High Potential	22 361	3,91
60	Gonçalo Mabunda	Mozambique	1975					•					To Watch	14 034	3,90
61	Sokari Douglas Camp	Nigeria	1958					•					High Potential	11 850	3,90
62	Lubaina Himid	Tanzania	1947	•				•	•				Undervalued Contemporary	0	3,85
63	Chief Jimoh Buraimoh	Nigeria	1943	•		•							Undervalued Contemporary	10 632	3,80
64	Djamel Tatah	Algeria	1959	•									High Potential	30 000	3,76
65	Zander Blom	South Africa	1982	•				•					High Potential	13 801	3,75
66	Faouzi Laatiris	Morocco	1958	•				•	•				Undervalued Contemporary	36 147	3,71
67	Dominique Zinkpe	Benin	1969	•	•			•					High Potential	25 480	3,71
68	Angus Taylor	South Africa	1970					•					High Potential	17 704	3,71

Source: Africa Art Market Report™

TOP 100 CONTEMPORY

N°	ARTIST	COUNTRY OF ORIGIN	DATES	Painting	Drawing	Collage	Print	Sculpture	Installation	Photography	Video	Performance	CATEGORY	TOTAL SALES 2016 (USD)	SCORE
69	Abderrahim Yamou	Morocco	1959	•								•	Undervalued Contemporary	16 985	3,71
70	Penny Siopis	South Africa	1953	•	•	•	•		•				Global Contemporary	120 339	3,69
71	Lucky Madlo Sibiya	South Africa	1942-1999	•			•	•					High Potential	26 503	3,66
72	Keith Alexander	Zimbabwe	1946-1998	•									High Potential	78 919	3,63
73	Jane Alexander	South Africa	1959					•					High Potential	5 688	3,60
74	Kay Hassan	South Africa	1956			•							Undervalued Contemporary	0	3,60
75	Olaku Abiodun	Nigeria	1958	•									High Potantial	40 352	3,56
76	Abdelazziz Zerrou	Morocco	1982		•			•					To Watch	22 646	3,56
77	Francis Uduh	Nigeria	1963					•					Undervalued Contemporary	16 718	3,56
78	Mohamed Hamidi	Morocco	1941	•									Undervalued Contemporary	28 440	3,51
79	Larbi Cherkaoui	Morocco	1972	•									To Watch	24 388	3,51
80	Beezy Bailey	South Africa	1962	•									High Potential	22 082	3,51
81	Kolade Oshinowo	Nigeria	1948	•									Undervalued Contemporary	19 514	3,51
82	Afifi Said	Morocco	1983	•									To Watch	15 658	3,51
83	Hennie (Christiaan) Niemann Snr	South Africa	1941	•									Undervalauted Contemporary	15 653	3,51
84	Yasmina Alaoui	Morocco	1977	•				•					To Watch	34 405	3,49
85	John Meyer	South Africa	1942	•									High Potential	47 679	3,47
86	Fouad Bellamine	Morocco	1950	•									High Potential	46 201	3,47
87	Conrad Nagel Doman Theys	South Africa	1940	•	•		•						High Potential	35 478	3,46
88	Kainebi Osahenye	Nigeria	1964	•									High Potential	29 425	3,46
89	Reuben Ugbine	Ghana	1956					•					Undervalued Contemporary	23 241	3,46
90	Bruce Clarke	South Africa	1959			•							High Potential	11 488	3,45
91	Ato Delaquis	Ghana	1945	•									High Potential	64 570	3,42
92	Willem Hendrik Adriaan Boshoff	South Africa	1951	•									High Potential	27 799	3,41
93	Rom Isichei	Nigeria	1966	•									Undervalued Contemporary	37 351	3,36
94	Peter Bongani Shange	South Africa	1951					•					Undervalued Contemporary	34 674	3,31
95	Bachir Demnati	Morocco	1946	•									High Potential	34 783	3,29
96	Nelson Makamo	South Africa	1982	•									To Watch	40 995	3,26
97	Babatunde Bunmi	Nigeria	1957					•					Undervalued Contemporary	29 769	3,16
98	Batoul S'Himi	Morocco	1974										To Watch	16 114	3,16
99	Dylan Lewis	South Africa	1964					•					High Potential	104 049	3,06
100	Amand Boua	Ivory Coast	1978	•		•							To Watch	11 599	2,95

Source: Africa Art Market Report™

TOP 5 LOTS SOLD AT AUCTION ALL CATEGORIES IN USD

N°	ARTIST	TITLE	PRICE	LOT	AUCTION HOUSE	MARKETPLACE	DATE
1	Marlene Dumas (1953)	Night Nurse, 1999-2000 Oil on canvas 200 x 100 cm	2 517 000	19	Phillips	New-York	May 8th 2016
2	Julie Mehretu (1970)	Excerpt (citadel), 2003 Acrylic and ink on canvas 81,5 x 137,4 cm	1 567 500	429	Christie's	New-York	November 16th 2016
3	Mahmoud Said (1897-1964)	L'Ile Heureuse, 1927 Oil on wood 80 x 70 cm	1 475 720	35	Bonhams	London	October 12th 2016
4	Omar El Nagdi (1931)	Sarajevo, 1992 Oil on canvas in three parts overall 315 x 1 080 cm	1 145 000	5	Christie's	Dubai	March 16th 2016
5	Irma Stern (1894-1966)	Arab with Jug, 1945 Oil on canvas 55,5 x 65 cm	1 118 082	30	Bonhams	London	September 14th 2016

Based on auction results from Bonhams, Christies, Phillips, Sotheby's, Art House, CMOOA, Cornette de St Cyr, Piasa and Strauss & Co. between January and December 2016 including buyer's premium. Source: Africa Art Market Report™

Source: Africa Art Market Report™

TOP 10 MODERN ART LOTS SOLD AT AUCTION IN USD

N°	ARTIST	TITLE	PRICE	LOT	AUCTION HOUSE	MARKETPLACE	DATE
1	Mahmoud Said (1897-1964)	L'île Heureuse, 1927 Oil on wood 80 x 70 cm	1 475 720	35	Bonhams	London	October 12th 2016
2	Omar El Nagdi (1931)	Sarajevo, 1992 Oil on canvas in three parts overall 315 x 1 080 cm	1 145 000	5	Christie's	Dubai	March 16th 2016
3	Irma Stern (1894-1966)	Arab with Jug, 1945 Oil on canvas 55,5 x 65 cm	1 118 082	30	Bonhams	London	September 14th 2016
4	Irma Stern (1894-1966)	Still Life with Lilies, 1947 Oil on canvas 83 x 76,5 cm	760 356	580	Strauss & Co	Cape Town	October 10th 2016
5	Mahmoud Said (1897-1964)	Le Nil à El Derr (Nubie) (The Nile in El Derr, Nubia), 1933 Oil on panel 62,3 x 79,3 cm	701 000	3	Christie's	Dubai	March 16th 2016
6	Mahmoud Mokhtar (1891-1934)	Al Amira (the Princess) Height 38 cm	669 718	25	Sotheby's	London	October 20th 2016
7	Hamed Ewais (1919-2011)	Al Aabour (The Crossing of the Suez Canal), 1974 Oil and wax crayons on canvas 123,4 x 98,8 cm	605 000	2	Christie's	Dubai	March 16th 2016
8	Alexis Preller (1911-1975)	Adam, 1969 Intaglio on fibre glass 183 x 91 cm	500 715	239	Strauss & Co	Johannesburg	November 7th 2016
9	Alexis Preller (1911-1975)	Space Angel, 1971 Oil and gesso on canvas 111 x 121 cm	484 024	234	Strauss & Co	Johannesburg	November 7th 2016
10	Irma Stern (1894-1966)	Still Life with Red Flowering Gum, 1938 Oil on canvas 74 x 81,5 cm	385 523	77	Bonhams	London	September 14th 2016

Based on auction results from Bonhams, Christies, Phillips, Sotheby's, Art House, CMOOA, Cornette de St Cyr, Piasa and Strauss & Co, between January and December 2016 including buyer's premium. Source: Africa Art Market Report™

TOP 10 CONTEMPORARY ART LOTS SOLD AT AUCTION IN USD

N°	ARTIST	TITLE	PRICE	LOT	AUCTION HOUSE	MARKETPLACE	DATE
1	Marlene Dumas (1953)	Night Nurse, 1999-2000 Oil on canvas 200 x 100 cm	2 517 000	19	Phillips	New-York	May 8th 2016
2	Julie Mehretu (1970)	Excerpt (citadel), 2003 Acrylic and ink on canvas 81,5 x 137,4 cm	1 567 500	429	Christie's	New-York	November 16th 2016
3	Njideka Akunyili Crosby (1983)	Drown, 2012 Acrylic, colored pencil and solvent transfer on paper 152.4 x 182.9 cm.	1 092 500	26	Sotheby's	New-York	November 17th 2016
4	Ibrahim El Anatsui (1944)	Exoke, 2013 Aluminum and copper wire 161.2 x 165.1 cm	845 000	442	Christie's	New-York	May 11th 2016
5	Marlene Dumas (1953)	Thepeeping Tom, 1994 Oil on canvas 69 x 50.2 cm	645 438	42	Sotheby's	London	June 28th 2016
6	Ibrahim El Anatsui (1944)	Used towel, 1999 carved, incised and paintedwood 81 x 250 cm (in 25 pieces)	256 822	49	Bonhams	London	May 25th 2016
7	Marlene Dumas (1953)	Erika, 1998 Ink and acrylic on paper 125 x 69.8 cm	175 000	402	Christie's	New-York	November 16th 2016
8	Marlene Dumas (1953)	Couple, 1996 mixed media on paper, in 2 parts each: 100 x 62.5 cm	166 609	125	Phillips	London	October 6th 2016
9	Wanguechi Mutu (1972)	Try Dismantling The Little Empire inside You, 2007 Ink, Mylar, pigment and photo collage, in 2 parts Overall: 242.5 x 264.1 cm	187 500	450	Sotheby's	New-York	November 18th 2016
10	Marlene Dumas (1953)	Green gloves, 1993 Watercolour and graphite on paper, (in 7parts) Each: 36x32cm	144 859	167	Sotheby's	London	Ferbruary 11th 2016

Based on auction results from Bonhams, Christies, Phillips, Sotheby's, Art House, CMOOA, Cornette de St Cyr, Piasa and Strauss & Co. between January and December 2016 including buyer's premium. Source: Africa Art Report™

Source: Africa Art Market Report™

MARKETPLACES

- Total lots sold at marketplaces by value in USD (%)
- Total lots sold at marketplaces by volume (%)
- Modern art total lots sold at marketplaces by value in USD (%)
- Modern art total lots sold at marketplaces by volume (%)
- Contemporary art total lots sold at marketplaces by value in USD (%)
- Contemporary art total lots sold at marketplaces by volume (%)

TOTAL LOTS SOLD AT MARKETPLACES BY VALUE IN USD (%)

JOBURG
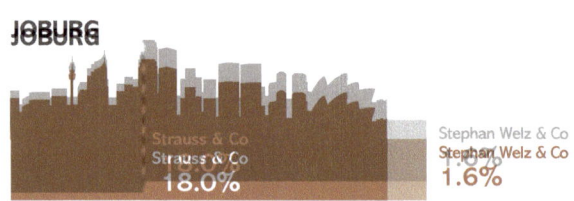
Strauss & Co 18.0%
Stephan Welz & Co 1.6%

MARRAKESH
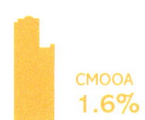
CMOOA 1.6%

CAPE TOWN
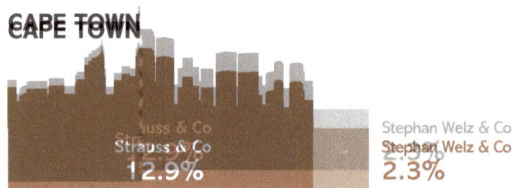
Strauss & Co 12.9%
Stephan Welz & Co 2.3%

CASABLANCA
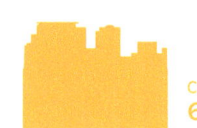
CMOOA 6.0%

LAGOS
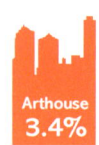
Arthouse 3.4%

LONDON
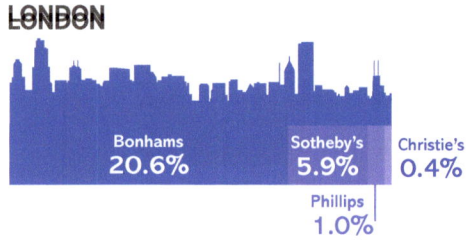
Bonhams 20.6%
Sotheby's 5.9%
Christie's 0.4%
Phillips 1.0%

PARIS
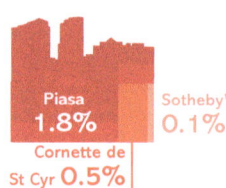
Piasa 1.8%
Sotheby's 0.1%
Cornette de St Cyr 0.5%

AMSTERDAM
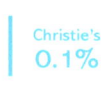
Christie's 0.1%

NEW YORK
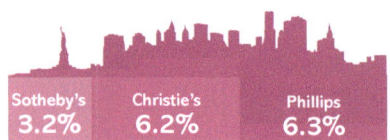
Sotheby's 3.2%
Christie's 6.2%
Phillips 6.3%

DUBAI
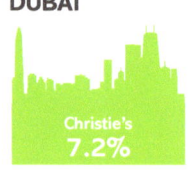
Christie's 7.2%

Source: Africa Art Market Report

TOTAL LOTS SOLD AT MARKETPLACES BY VOLUME (%)

JOBURG
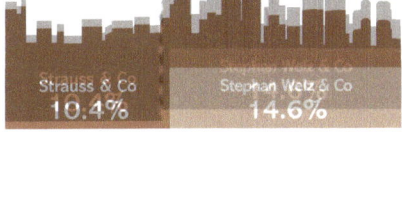
Strauss & Co 46.5%
Stephan Welz & Co 7.3%

MARRAKESH
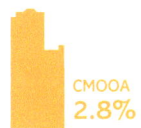
CMOOA 1.6%

CAPE TOWN
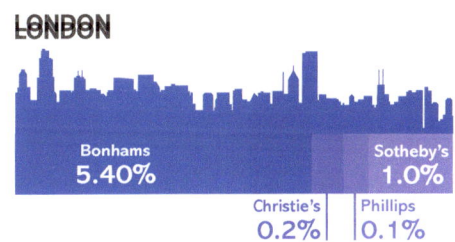
Strauss & Co 10.4%
Stephan Welz & Co 14.6%

CASABLANCA
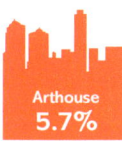
CMOOA 2.8%

LAGOS
Arthouse 5.7%

LONDON
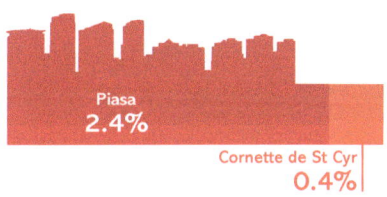
Bonhams 5.40%
Sotheby's 1.0%
Christie's 0.2%
Phillips 0.1%

PARIS
Piasa 2.4%
Cornette de St Cyr 0.4%

NEW YORK
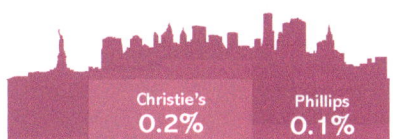
Christie's 0.2%
Phillips 0.1%

DUBAI
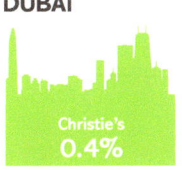
Christie's 0.4%
Others 0.4%

Source: Africa Art Market Report

MODERN ART TOTAL LOTS SOLD AT MARKETPLACES BY VALUE IN USD (%)

JOBURG

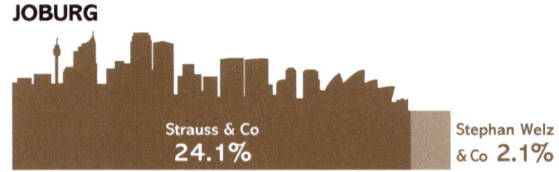

Strauss & Co 24.1% Stephan Welz & Co 2.1%

CASABLANCA

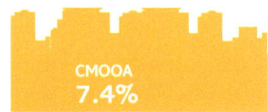

CMOOA 7.4%

CAPE TOWN

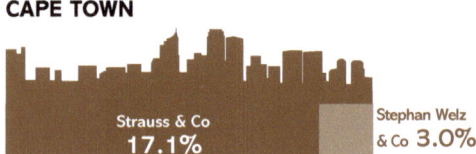

Strauss & Co 17.1% Stephan Welz & Co 3.0%

LAGOS

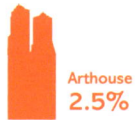

Arthouse 2.5%

LONDON

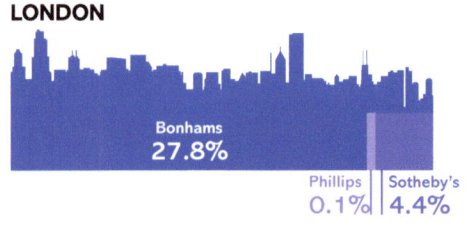

Bonhams 27.8% Phillips 0.1% Sotheby's 4.4%

PARIS

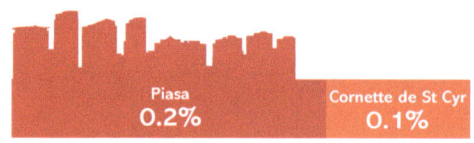

Piasa 0.2% Cornette de St Cyr 0.1%

DUBAI

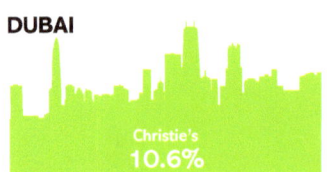

Christie's 10.6%

Source: Africa Art Market Report™

MODERN ART TOTAL LOTS SOLD AT MARKETPLACES BY VOLUME (%)

JOBURG

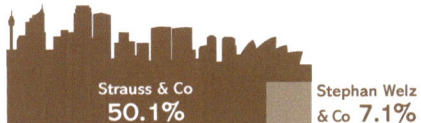

Strauss & Co **50.1%** Stephan Welz & Co **7.1%**

CASABLANCA

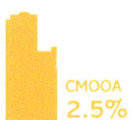

CMOOA **2.5%**

CAPE TOWN

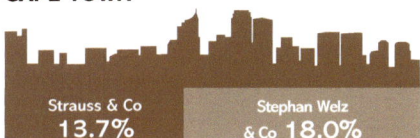

Strauss & Co **13.7%** Stephan Welz & Co **18.0%**

LAGOS

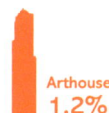

Arthouse **1.2%**

LONDON

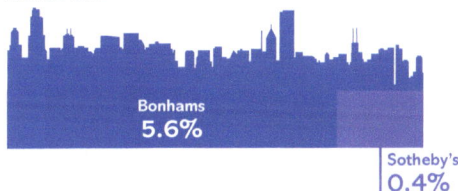

Bonhams **5.6%** Sotheby's **0.4%**

PARIS

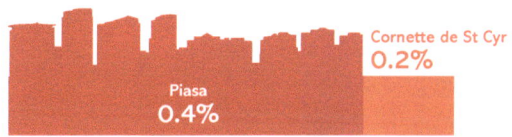

Piasa **0.4%** Cornette de St Cyr **0.2%**

DUBAI

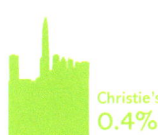

Christie's **0.4%**

Source: Africa Art Market Report™

CONTEMPORARY ART TOTAL LOTS SOLD AT MARKETPLACES BY VALUE IN USD (%)

JOBURG
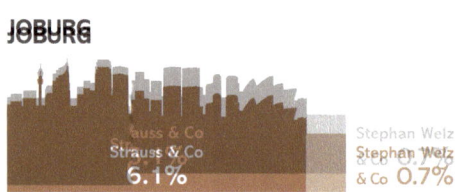
Strauss & Co 6.1%
Stephan Welz & Co 0.7%

MARRAKESH
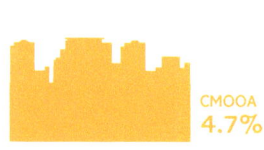
CMOOA 4.7%

CAPE TOWN
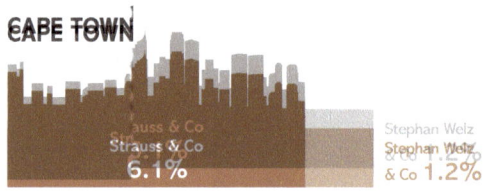
Strauss & Co 6.1%
Stephan Welz & Co 1.2%

CASABLANCA
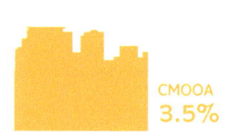
CMOOA 3.5%

LAGOS
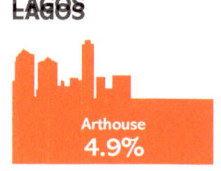
Arthouse 4.9%

LONDON
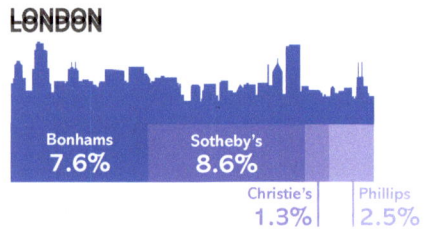
Bonhams 7.6%
Sotheby's 8.6%
Christie's 1.3%
Phillips 2.5%

PARIS
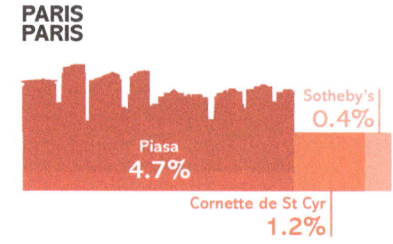
Piasa 4.7%
Sotheby's 0.4%
Cornette de St Cyr 1.2%

NEW YORK
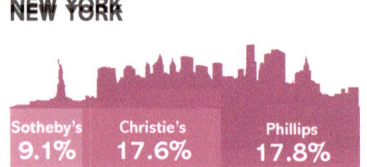
Sotheby's 9.1%
Christie's 17.6%
Phillips 17.8%

DUBAI
Christie's 1.0%

AMSTERDAM
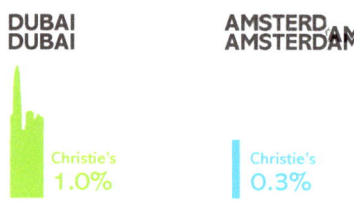
Christie's 0.3%

Source: Africa Art Market Report

CONTEMPORARY ART TOTAL LOTS SOLD AT MARKETPLACES BY VOLUME (%)

JOBURG
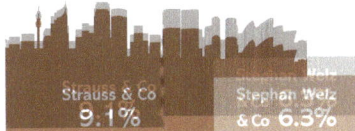
Strauss & Co 9.1%
Stephan Welz & Co 6.3%

MARRAKESH
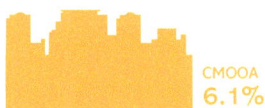
CMOOA 6.1%

CAPE TOWN
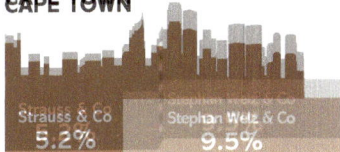
Strauss & Co 5.2%
Stephan Welz & Co 9.5%

CASABLANCA

CMOOA 3.3%

LAGOS
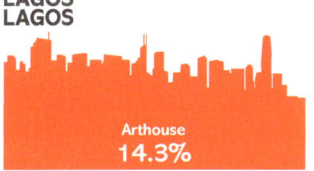
Arthouse 14.3%

LONDON
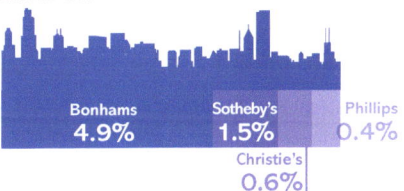
Bonhams 4.9%
Sotheby's 1.5%
Phillips 0.4%
Christie's 0.6%

PARIS
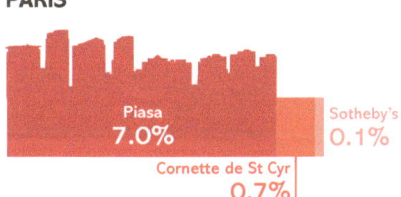
Piasa 7.0%
Sotheby's 0.1%
Cornette de St Cyr 0.7%

NEW YORK
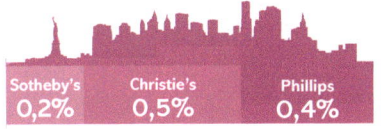
Sotheby's 0,2%
Christie's 0,5%
Phillips 0,4%

DUBAI
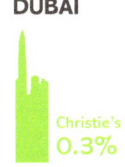
Christie's 0.3%

AMSTERDAM
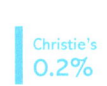
Christie's 0.2%

Source: Africa Art Market Report

HOW TO ANSWER QUESTIONS RELATED TO

conservation, restoration, dating, characterization or authentication of art objects

**Analytical research unit
which applies history of art and the most suitable
and modern physico-chemical techniques**

contact@africartmarket.today

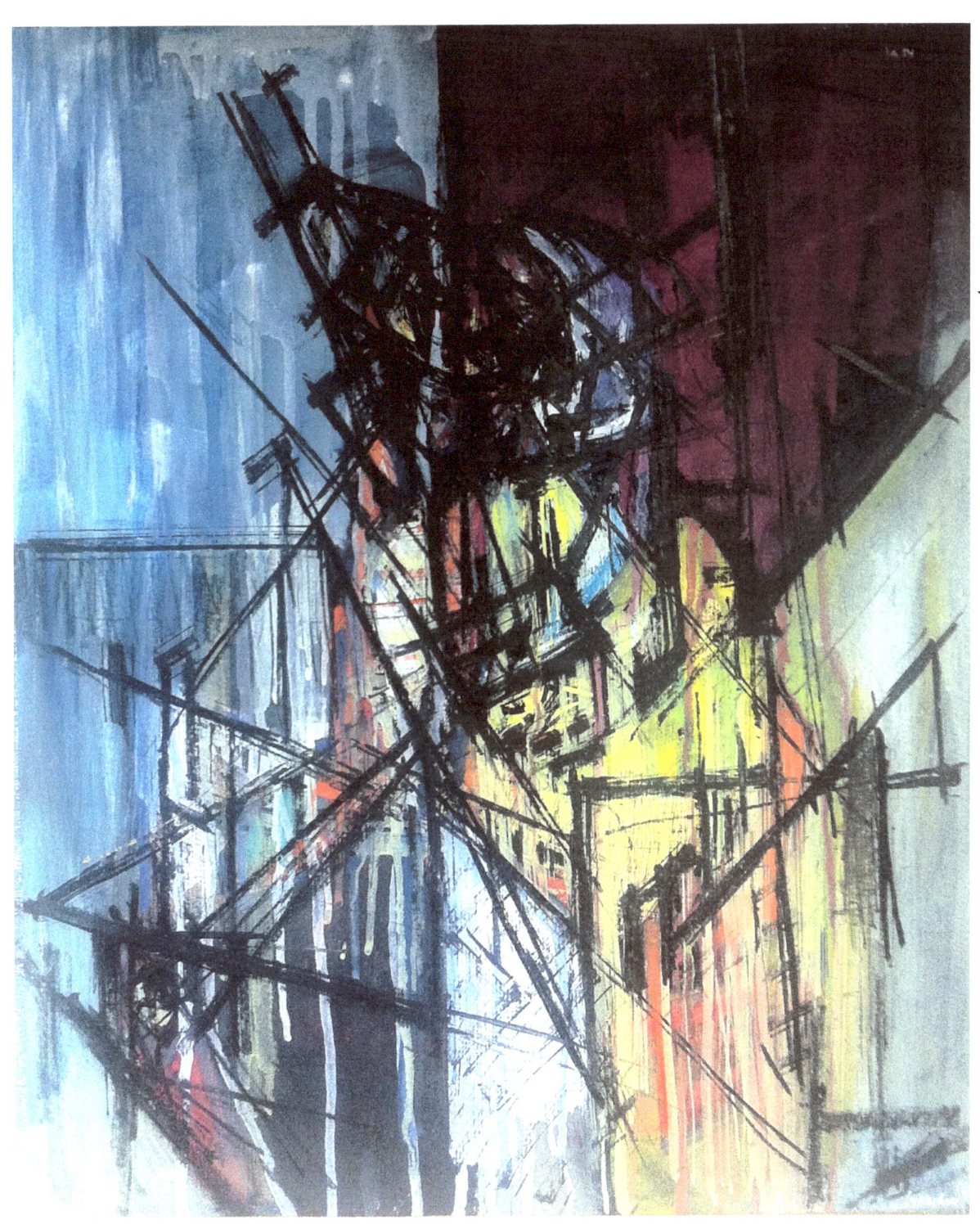

ABDALLAH Benanteur (b.1931)
Le Baiser (The Kiss), 1954
Oil on panel, 65.2x54.2cm - Court. private collection

Auction house market share

- Auction houses total lots sold by value in USD (%)
- Auction houses total lots sold by volume (%)

AUCTION HOUSES TOTAL LOTS SOLD BY VALUE IN USD (%)

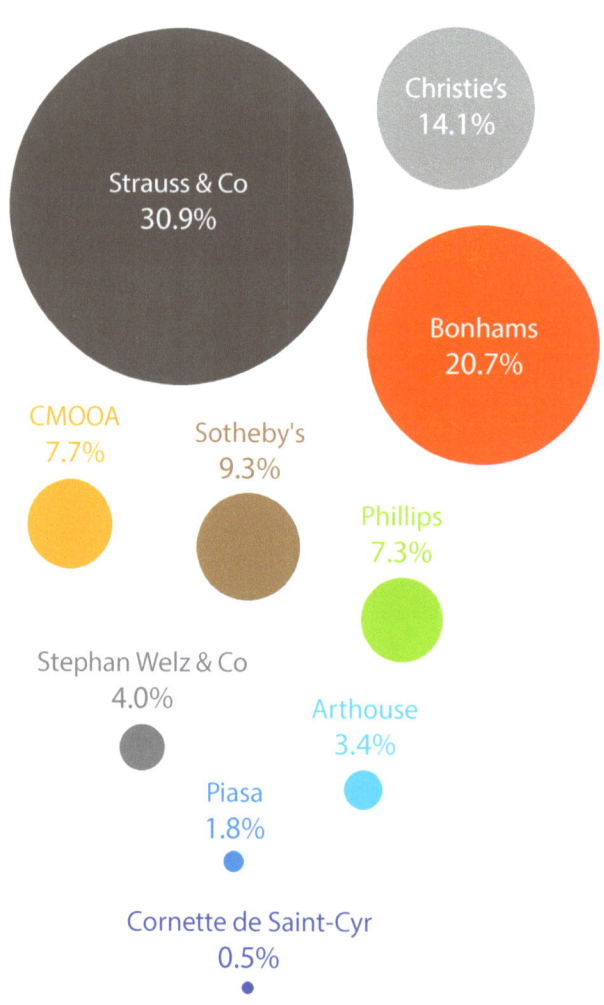

Source: Africa Art Market Report™

AUCTION HOUSES TOTAL LOTS SOLD BY VOLUME (%)

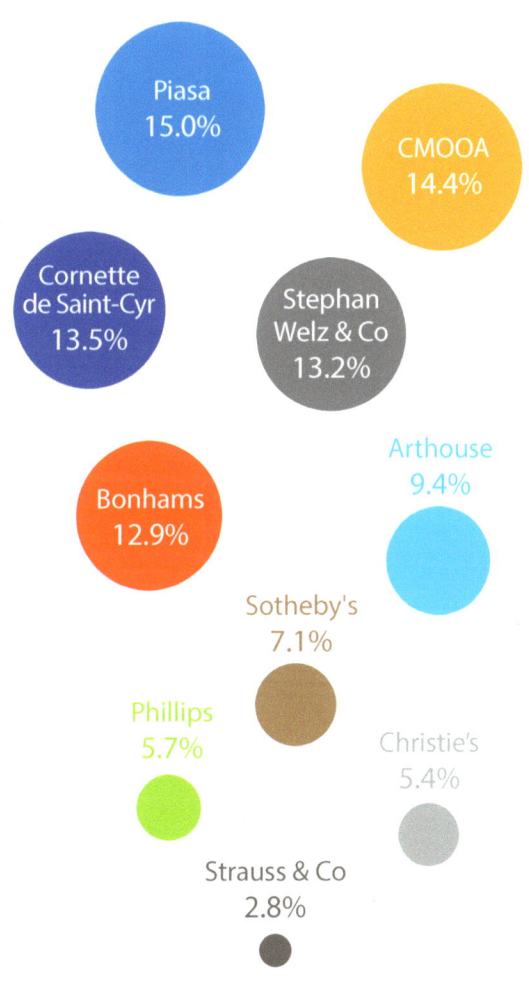

Source: Africa Art Market Report™

THE DIASPORA AND THE GLOBAL ART DISCOURSE

- Overview by Osei G. Kofi
- Julia Grosse & Yvette Mutumba, co founders of Contemporary And
- Tumelo Mosaka, art curator
- Mimi Errol, journalist
- Mustapha Orif, art dealer
- Lionel Manga, art critic
- Nii Andrew, art reviewer

OVERVIEW

Osei G. Kofi

IT'S A NEW DAY

The African Diaspora is a worldwide church, covering millions of peoples across the seven continents, of a plethora of cultures, and whose ancestral DNA is etched into and resonates the Mother Continent - the Homeland. As an operational tool the term is applied to first-second generation Africans with national or constitutional idendity outside Africa.

A remarkable innovation on the art scene is that many creatives have chosen to shuttle between the Homelandand Outer lands. In other words, the entire world is their inspiration, their canvas, their clay, their stone. Cameroonian Barthélémy Toguo, Ghanaian Owusu Ankomah and Kenyan Wangechi Mutu are among the exemplars.

Africa is the most recent region, barely two decades ago, to enter the global art space and its premium sub-spaces of museums, galleries, corporate & private collections, fairs and auction houses. The early years saw significant tension between the Diaspora and Homeland artists and curators. The Diaspora operated within the core market, namely, Europe and North America. Logically, they were better placed to tap into the opportunities on offer. Nonetheless, they came under criticism from artists and gallerists in the Homeland who accused the impresarios of westernart institutions and private galleries of favouring art labelled "African contemporary" but which were often anything but. Too often the art aped uncomfortably the styles and tastes of the West, especially so in installation and performance art.

There were those who argued, art is art and has no specific ID or geographic boundary. Right, up to a degree. Some might take umbrage at the "African" tag to "contemporary." However, geo-localization is valued more for its inherent creative distinctiveness than its perceived negative connotation. Deny it at own peril. Distinctiveness isn't bad. It's not ghettoization. The fact is western art, ancient and modern, has distinct geo-social DNA. Ditto, Oriental, Latin American or Asian art within the global spectrum. A Japanese painting like a Rembrandt without a Japanese cultural inflexion is soon submerged, to vanish without trace. Malian Seydou Keita's photographs, shot in conditions that would befuddle a non-African photographer, exude a cadence, a mojo, that would escape other practitioners of the art form who hadn't been weaned in Keita's Mande-Bambara environment.

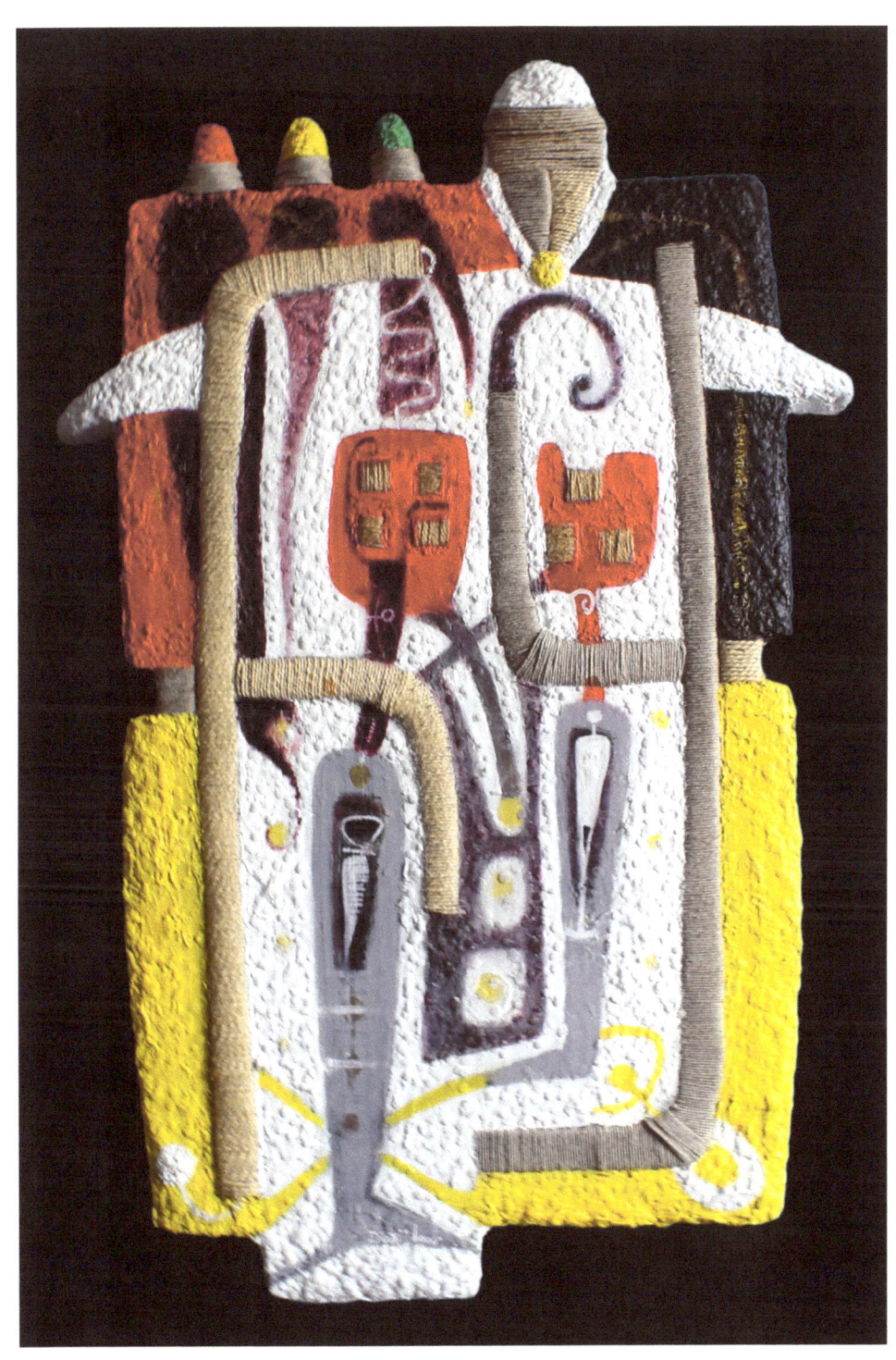

Ernest Dükü (b.1958)
Entre nous histoire elle court, 2003
mixed media, 91x62x5 cm - Court. the artist

Julia Grosse & Yvette Mutumba
co founders of Contemporary And

Julia Grosse and Yvette Mutumba founded Contemporary And (C&), the online platform for international art from African perspectives, in Berlin in 2013. The duo were invited by Noah Horowitz, when he was director of the Armory Show in New York, to curate the Focus: African Perspectives section of the 2016 edition of the fair features 13 galleries. This followed on from the focus on China in 2014 and on the Middle East, North Africa and the Mediterranean in 2015. They are the first women to curate an edition of Armory Focus in its seven-year history.

How did the invitation to curate Focus: African Perspectives at the 2016 Armory Show arise?
Noah Horowitz approached us, following a recommendation from some curators, and said that the Armory would like to put a focus on the African continent. That particular focus didn't interest us, because for us, at C&, there's no such thing as African art but art from African perspectives, such as an artist in Nairobi with parents from Ghana or an artist in London who comes from Tanzania. A painter from Johannesburg does completely different things from a performance artist from Cairo. But there's still this tendency to put this overall "African art" label on very diverse practices in Africa and the diaspora. So we told Noah that we would love to curate this section but with a focus on African perspectives, including galleries from African cities and from the diaspora in Paris and London.

How did you envision Focus: African Perspectives?
We had this ideal scenario in mind that visitors would enter the Focus area, which was connected to another hall, and not realise that they were entering a section with art from Africa. We wanted them to see art mostly by very young artists and not see something typically African. There were no hints, like masks or patterns. From the feedback we got, we think people understood that there's no such thing as African art but many styles and approaches.

What was your concept?
It was to show youngsters together with old masters. We started from the artists that we wanted to include and then approached their galleries. So we asked the galleries to focus on one artist and do solo presentations instead of having five or six artists squeezed into a small, overloaded space. From a curatorial perspective, it was great and looked like a little exhibition show curated by a gallery. But we recognised that it was a big risk to ask the galleries to bring one artist only. But the Focus was financially successful, too, because all the galleries sold work. It would have been horrible if the concept had been aesthetically pleasing but not a single gallery had been able to sell something. Besides the galleries that spotlighted very young contemporary artists, we included two galleries, Vigo Gallery and October Gallery in London, that showed older masters: the Sudanese artist Ibrahim El-Salahi (b.1930) and Aubrey Williams (b.1926-d.1990). It was an honour for us that their galleries agreed to take part because these artists' pieces cost several hundred thousand dollars. Our reason for including them is that at C& we emphasise that contemporary art from Africa and the diaspora didn't just pop up 10 years ago. There are diverse African histories and modern art existed decades ago. The galleries with the young artists were in the middle of the floor plan, with the old masters on either side.

What were the strongest sales?

There was one painting by El-Salahi that was almost $1 million. There were also some important museum acquisitions. For instance, Blank project, Cape Town sold sold out their entire booth dedicated to South African artist Turiya Magadlela. Also The Studio Museum in Harlem, New York acquired a piece by Turiya Magadlela.

How did visitors respond to the Focus section?

Visitors were surprised to discover works, like photography and painting, by young artists that didn't fall into their expectations of African perspectives. The artists weren't big names in the art world context and their works weren't stereotypical. It was surprising for the black American visitors to see so much art from Africa and the diaspora in Europe that they weren't aware of, in contrast to some of the black American artists being so huge and established. Everyone knows El Anatsui but this was a great platform to present the younger generation to potential collectors.

What feedback did you get from the galleries that participated in the Focus section?

The galleries, Addis Fine Art, from Addis Ababa in Ethiopia or Omenka Gallery from Lagos in Nigeria all said that it was worth doing because normally they can't afford to be in an art fair such as the Armory and they wanted to be seen and present their artists. A Seattle-based gallery, Mariane Ibrahim Gallery, which was part of Focus: African Perspectives, was accepted to participate in the main fair this year and won the prize for the best booth, which made us happy.

What do you think of these country or region-focused sections in fairs and exhibitions, such as the Africa-themed exhibitions?

It's great for the artists who wouldn't normally get the chance to have their work exhibited in Europe or the US. But it's a trend-driven interest: a few years ago it was India, then China and maybe next it will be Australia. But at C&, we look at what we do with a long-term, sustainable vision. The problem of putting this "African art" label on everything is that the same names keep coming up.

How are the dreams and ambitions of artists from the African diaspora changing?

If you talk to young artists working in Nairobi or Johannesburg, they're not dreaming of finally having a show in London. That's not the trend any more, which you may have had with artists now in their late fifties who live in Belgium or London. The younger generation is interested in working on the ground in their own cities, starting art spaces or residency programmes. Europe or the western art world isn't the paradise or goal any longer. Thinking that once you've made it in London or New York, you've made it an artist, is less common now. Young artists have the possibility to travel a lot and do a residency in New York or Rotterdam, or stay in Berlin for a year. Over the last 10 years, there's been a tendency for them to return to work in their own city's art scene afterwards and to recognise that there's a lot going on beyond Berlin and London. A Ghanian artist might have a show in New York and then go back to Accra to establish their artistic infrastructure. We were in Congo in May, where we talked to a very established painter in his sixties. He told us, "I'm not interested in moving to Paris, I have my infrastructure and my colleagues here, and I'm about to start a residency programme and build a house in the garden where artists from other African cities can stay." So it's not just the youngsters who are interested in staying on the ground instead of going to Europe.

What projects are you working on?

We've just published our first book, featuring some of the features published on C& in the last four years. The latest print edition of our magazine, focusing on education, was launched in collaboration with documenta in June. We're also running critical writing workshops, the third of which will be in Harare, Zimbabwe, in September. Next year we're launching an extension of C&, focusing on the relationship between Africa and South America.

Tumelo Mosaka
Art curator

Tumelo Mosaka is a contemporary art curator whose projects have explored global and transnational artistic production, especially from Africa, the Caribbean and North America, and have examined subjects such as racial injustice, migration and identity. After being associate curator of exhibitions at the Brooklyn Museum in New York and contemporary art curator at the Krannert Art Museum in Champaign, Illinois, Mosaka returned to South Africa in late 2016 and became chief art curator of Cape Town Art Fair.

What was your goal when you became Cape Town Art Fair's chief art curator and what was your vision for the Tomorrows/Today section?

My goal was to enter into a conversation with artists from Africa again and explore how Cape Town can be a gateway to the world, especially for contemporary art. My vision for Tomorrows/Today was to offer lesser known artists a platform to participate in that dialogue. I was looking locally and internationally for under-represented artists making cutting-edge works and for whom the fair would play a pivotal role in providing exposure. I had conversations with many artists and galleries about how to make this section different. Curating at a fair is very different from curating museum exhibitions and requires constant negotiation between galleries and artists. What kept it real was the artists' enthusiasm and their dynamic works.

Which artists from the diaspora did you work with?

Marcia Kure from Nigeria who lives in New York and is represented by Bloom Art Lagos in Nigeria, Joel Andrianomearisoa from Madagascar who lives in Paris and is represented by Sabrina Amrina Gallery from Madrid, and Maurice Mbikayi from Congo who lives in Cape Town and is represented by Gallery Momo in Cape Town and Johannesburg. I was looking for works in different media and themes, and by artists in different age groups. Besides looking at geographical location, I was interested in how they use symbols to provoke, inform and construct alternative histories. Take Mbikayi's photographs, which make a commentary on technological waste, urbanism and popular culture in the Congo.

How does working in the diaspora influence an artist's work?

Because artists move from place to place, their histories aren't linear but are far more complex and don't necessarily respond to their place of birth. What interested me was how they negotiate multiple spaces and identities. Artists are very sensitive to how place and identity inform personal narrative and reflect their locality. As a curator, I'm always thinking about how the message is communicated and relates to the everyday experience.

How have your curatorial experiences in the US shaped your perspective on the diaspora?

There isn't one diaspora but rather several which are defined by our relationship to people and places. Being from elsewhere entails being in contact with home and family while creating new communities in new spaces and redefining our existence. The diaspora is about the experience of building bridges, maintaining relations and finding a common ground with others, as migration remains a constant reality today. So it's about understanding the rupture and distance and reshaping one's way of life.

What effect do you think the African diaspora has had on the art world?

It's huge. I don't think there's anywhere in the world where there aren't any black people today. Maybe Antartica! We're talking about a history of forced and voluntary migration over centuries, which has resulted in generations of people living everywhere. The geographical distance and the historical distortions have meant that Africa has continued to be this misunderstood place. Most of the west wants to see Africa in a past image and yet contemporary Africa is very much in keeping with how the modern world has developed. With such a large diaspora, more artists are not only demystifying old narratives but resisting any stereotypical representation.

There are a lot of artists living and working in different parts of the world that have gained international attention and propose a different understanding of what "Africa" is today. It's a challenge since the canon of art and representation of black people needs to be totally overhauled. At Cape Town Art Fair, you can see the scale and scope of creativity that's being produced within and outside of the continent. The fair is about bringing all this to the forefront and creating a visible dialogue about these issues.

How would you describe the impact of the diaspora in South Africa?

Under apartheid, black South Africans grew up as foreigners in our own land. So the experience of internal immigration and temporary residency is all too familiar. The impact of the diaspora is also about understanding that our experience isn't unique in terms of systematic suppression.

The ongoing dialogue of the diaspora presents the potential to address issues and offer new realities that are yet to be realised. In South Africa, we can begin to talk about race and inequality in a different way, which is much more complicated than addressing them in a black-and-white, racial dynamic.

What do you think of the so-called boom in contemporary art from Africa?

I keep hearing about a boom in Africa but I don't believe it. I agree that contemporary African art has been steadily receiving more attention, partly thanks to people like the curator Okwui Enwezor who have championed the cause over time. To claim that there's a boom is an exaggeration as many artists from Africa continue to be marginalized or only considered within the context of Africa.

Secondly, the market has not responded in the same manner when it comes to pricing works by these artists. Institutions are only now beginning to realize the gap they have in their collections when they talk about global art. Why is it so hard to accept African artists as being contemporary? Why is there the need to qualify them as African in this day and age?

Mimi ERROL
Journalist

The diaspora, in all its senses, has played and continues to play an important role in artistic production in Ivory Coast. This is true for all sectors of the art system, from galleries and collectors to the production of artworks, art criticism and the academic teaching of fine art.

However, the notion of the diaspora is nuanced, especially when one is talking about Ivory Coast. Indeed, one cannot talk about an Ivorian diaspora in the same way as one talks about a Senegalese diaspora with the Mourides – a diaspora based on something that is both about community and religion and takes root in the host country. Equally, it is not a diaspora that has come about through deportation, even though this played a leading role in the development of contemporary art in Ivory Coast, especially with the Negro-Caribbean School and artists such as Serge Hélénon, the artist/painter and teacher at Abidjan's National Fine Arts School from 1976-1983. He was at the inception of what became known as the School of Abidjan and the Vohou-Vohou movement. At the end of the 1960s, there was a reflux of emancipation, authenticity and black civil rights movements that followed those that happened in the US and the Caribbean.

In this context, it is necessary to highlight the highly important patronage role played by the West Indian governor Guy Nairay, who President Félix Houphouët-Boigny retained as an adviser following Ivory Coast's independence. He was the natural godfather of all the activities of Ivory Coast's artists through the Pen Club, which he set up in order to accompany their exhibition projects. All this took place in an era when there were hardly any real art galleries in Ivory Coast.

Furthermore, the most important Ivorian diaspora, which determined the principle by which different waves of immigration evolved until 1981 when François Mitterrand came to power in France, was sparked by Félix Houphouët-Boigny. Before becoming the first president of an independent Ivory Coast, Houphouët-Boigny was a deputy of the assembly (when Ivory Coast was still part of the French Federation of West Africa) and had the visionary idea of sending 146 young people from upper Ivory Coast (now Burkina Faso) and lower Ivory Coast abroad. The aim of this adventure was to train them in all domains of society. Most of these young people returned to Ivory Coast after their studies and constituted the first wave of high-level officials of post-independence Ivory Coast. This adventure, called the Adventure 1946, provided Ivory Coast with a major player in Ivory Coast's art scene: Dalouman Simone, who created the country's first art gallery, Galerie Arts Pluriels.

However, it is worth mentioning that in addition to the young scholars from Ivory Coast that there were some young Ivorians who made individual trips to France that were financed by their affluent parents. The most emblematic, in the domain of visual arts, of these migrants that went to France was Christian Lattier (1925-1978). The son of a doctor, it was Lattier who instigated the era of Ivorian contemporary art – art that unfolds before our eyes and gives pre-eminence to an idea rather than the materiality of the work. Indeed, Lattier's voluminous sculptures, which he made with his bare hands with materials like iron wire and sisal rope, overturned all the conventional techniques known to sculptural art. He justified his concept by saying, "If I'd have made them from wood, I'd have been accused of copying my ancestors. If I'd have carved from stone, people would have said that I was copying the white man. So I had to find something new." From this refusal to imitate, an innovative work was born. The fact that he won the Grand Prix of Visual Art in the first festival of black art in Dakar, beating 219 other candidates from Africa, Europe and the US, gives an idea of the level of his artistic approach. The award was given to the artist "who, according to the rules, has attained – by deeply taking root in the black world – an artistic and human expression of a high level, regardless of the technique." Notably, Lattier participated in exhibitions with Pablo Picasso, Salvador Dali and Bernard Buffet.

Another fact that adds to the Ivorians' tendency of not having a strong diaspora is underscored by Hélène Bergues in her 1973 report titled "The immigration of black African workers in France and particularly in the Parisian region". On page 62, she describes how the countries with strong immigration are those where the land is poor and where the possibility of making use of arable land is short-lived. This is not the case of Ivory Coast which, on the contrary, was the welcoming land of choice for all the migrants from the West African sub-region, which faced this difficulty of non-arable land.

From this, one can understand the delayed date, in 1970, of the ratification of the "Treaty on co-operation", signed in Paris in 1961, between France and the Ivory Coast, which countries such as Mali, Mauritania and Senegal made between 1963 and 1964. The agreements also made a distinction between the immigrants that wanted to exercise a salaried activity and those that did not, and specified that the volume of migrants arriving from black Africa mentioned the relatively low number coming from Ivory Coast.

The first wave of the pre-colonial diaspora determined the principle of immigration, which was essentially that of students and therefore temporary and inscribed in the period of studies. This continued until the French presidential election of 1981, which was won by the Socialist François Mitterrand. Mitterrand's new government proceeded to carry out a huge regularisation of foreigners who had been living in an irregular situation.

This situation enabled artists such as Ouattara Watt to officially practice their profession. This was prior to Watt, an artist-painter, meeting Jean-Michel Basquiat in 1988. Living in New York since 1988, he is a figurehead of art from Ivory Coast and is the standard bearer in international contests. He has participated in three editions of the Venice Biennale – he is one of four artists representing the Ivory Coast Pavilion in 2017 – and in one edition of Documenta. His visits to Ivory Coast represent an opportunity for young artists to learn about how he got into the ferocious American art market through actively seeking out encounters.

Equally remarkable about this diaspora is the artist Ernest Düku. Born in 1958 in Bouake, he studied at Abidjan's National Fine Arts School and has been living in Paris since 1982. Qualified as an architect and holding a degree in sciences of art and philosophy from Paris Panthéon Sorbonne, he divides his time between France, his host country, and the Ivory Coast, his country of origin. When in Ivory Coast, he teaches interior architecture at INSAAC (Abidjan's fine arts school). His part-time presence is a considerable contribution, not only because of the quality of his pictorial production and the pedagogical level of his classes, but also because of the quality and depth of his interventions in the formal and informal debates around art.

Dorris Haron Kasco, born in Ivory Coast, is the first Ivorian photographer to have presented his images in an art gallery. His exhibition, titled "La Femme Masquée" (The Masked Woman), showed all of the woman except her face and took place at Galerie Arts Pluriels. His book, "Les fous d'Abidjan", was published by Revue Noire, the

French publishing house, in 1994 following his exhibition, "Ils sont fous, on s'en fout" in Abidjan the year before. The political-military crisis that hit Ivory Coast in 2002 interrupted his comings and goings between his native country and France, leading him to concentrate on teaching at Montpellier's fine arts school. Since 2011, when the crisis ended, he has been returning to Ivory Coast nearly every year in order to establish a collaboration with INSAAC, where he organises workshops for the students. Kasco co-organised the photography exhibition, "Bazouam", in spring 2017 in the historic city of Grand-Bassam with the photographer/writer Armand Gauz. Gauz has been living and working between France and Ivory Coast since 1999. His novel "Debout-Payé", published by Le nouvel Attila, was the best first French novel of 2014, according to "Lire" magazine's "best books of the year" rating. Through their exhibition in an open-air gallery on the road, Kasco and Gauz sought to break down barriers to art and make it more accessible.

In the medium of photography, the career of Ananias Léki Dago typifies what the Ivorian diaspora has brought about in the last decade. After studying photography at Abidjan's INSAAC, he went to live in France at the beginning of the 2000s. After relocating, he travelled around the African continent, questioning its multicultural aspects in the urban context. This included observing the shebeens (drinking taverns) in Johannesburg's townships in South Africa, the rickshaws in Bamako in Mali and the corrugated iron sheets defining the roofs of Nairobi in Kenya. He extended this experience to the town of Cotonou in Benin and its motorbike-taxis, called Zémidjan. This project led to his work entering the collection of the prestigious Philadelphia Museum of Art, which acquired an important collection of 20 photographs from his series on Johannesburg, Nairobi and Bamako. His success has brought immense national pride.

Then there's the sculptor Jems Robert Koko Bi, the most emblematic sculptor from Ivory Coast. Born in 1966, he studied at the Institut National Supérieur des Arts et de l'Action Culturelle (INSAAC) in Abidjan, where he trained under the sculptor Klaus Simon in a studio initiated by the Goethe Institute. Subsequently, he received a DAAD scholarship in 1997 allowing him to further his studies at Kunstakademie Düsseldorf in Düsseldorf, Germany, where his professor was Klaus Rinke, a friend and colleague of Joseph Beuys. Here he gained a Master's degree. Currently based between Essen and Abidjan, Koko Bi establishes a link between the west and Africa in his work. His international career serves as a nice reminder of how Ivory Coast's contemporary era opened with the sculptor Christian Lattier.

If Abidjan has become the scene of a contemporary art market, despite the crises that have slowed its pace, this is partly thanks to the movement of young people from Ivory Coast in the diaspora. These artists have enjoyed an artistic career that has opened them up to the art markets in Europe and the US. Also worth mentioning are the young, motivated collectors that have arisen from the diaspora. One such example is Georges Moulo, 47, who has been buying pieces by young emerging artists. Educated in Switzerland and with parents based in Canada, he has a collection estimated between CFA Francs 20-30 million (US$36 000-72 000). It is mainly composed of works by young artists such as Sanogo Souleymane, known as Pachard, and Agoh Stefan Mobio in the diaspora in France, Youssouf De Kimbirila in Canada and others based in Ivory Coast. From a critical perspective, the critic Franck Hermann Ekra has made a valid contribution.

He is the first winner of the AICA (International Association of Art Critics) prize for a young critic who has published pertinent articles on Ivory Coast's art scene in the respected French magazine "Art Press". On the commercial front, Laurence Aphing Kouassi has been trying to get businesses involved in art after completing her marketing studies in Lyon and Canada.

Inversely, there are the artists living in the Ivory Coast, such as Aboudia who is represented by Ethan Cohen in New York and Armand Boua represented by Jack Bell Gallery in London.

Mustapha ORIF
Art dealer

Algeria's art market began in the mid-1980s thanks to two Algerian galleries: Galerie Xenia, which closed in 1987, and Galerie Issiakhem, which was renamed Isma in 1989. They were joined by Galerie M, which closed in 1992. The market, which circulated around these three galleries, grew until 1992/1993 when it was suddenly interrupted by political upheavals from 1992-2000.

The market picked up after 2002, shyly at first before growing steadily ever since. It is mainly dominated by unoriginal works; modern and contemporary art and historical Orientalism art (19th and early 20th century) occupy a minor place for different reasons. The rather conservative profile of the buyers explains the confidential character of the Algerian modern and contemporary art market, while the limited offer of historical Orientalism art in Algeria explains its smaller part. However, the current trend is heading towards an inversion of this. Modern art, represented by artists such as M'hamed Issiakhem, Baya Mahieddine and Mohammed Khadda, is drawing more interest, mainly due to their works entering public sales at the auction houses Gros & Delettrez, Aguttes, Ader and Million at Drouot in Paris, at Sotheby's in Doha and at Christie's in Dubai, where strong prices have been fetched.

Meanwhile, Christie's Dubai is boosting contemporary artists, such as Rachid Koraïchi, Ahmed Ben Bella, Abdallah Benanteur, Rachid Khimoune, Kader Attia and Djamel Tatah. The success of these artists has attracted the attention of Algerian collectors who had previously only been interested in Orientalism and unoriginal works. The prices of artworks by these artists are beginning to go up in Algiers, indicating how the contemporary art market is taking off.

Since 2005/2006, the art market has been articulated around 10 galleries, mostly located in Algiers. These galleries are mostly managed by young people who evidently enjoy their profession and seek to promote young Algerian artists. The exhibitions that they organise are regular and increasingly more numerous. However, it would seem that the artistic dynamic does not translate into commercial vitality; this is undoubtedly due to the profile of the buyers but also due to the young galleries' lack of experience.

Al Marhoon Gallery, a young gallery in Algiers, seems to have a professional approach. Besides organising exhibitions, it participates in fairs abroad, such as Art Dubai and AKAA in Paris, where it can present its artists to a foreign audience. Furthermore, its well-designed website enhances the visibility of its artists.

Another gallery, Seen Art Gallery, seems promising as does the alternative structure, Les Ateliers Sauvages, which takes a particular interest in young artists, such as the group Picturie Générale (Mourad Krinah, Walid Bouchouchi and Youcef Krache).

Alongside these galleries, the MAMA (Musée Public National d'Art Moderne et Contemporain – the national museum of modern and contemporary art) has played a central role since its inauguration in 2007. It has earnt a reputation for the quality of its exhibitions, which have enabled the Algerian public, including collectors, to discover Algerian modern and contemporary art and the artists of the diaspora, as well as those hailing from Africa and the Arab world.

The five exhibitions on African creation in 2009, coinciding with the second Panafrican festival that year, sparked a keen interest in art, Africa and the Arab world, encouraging artists – especially the young generation – to go and see what was happening in Arab and African cultures, thus broadening their artistic outlook.

Websites such as founoune. com also contribute to a better legibility of art in Algeria, as do the sections on art in the daily press. The efforts of the galleries, along with the interest of auction houses such as Christie's and Sotheby's, have strengthened the idea that it is perhaps time for Algerian collectors to look more closely at Algeria's artistic heritage. This indicates a progression from buying to decorate one's interior to the desire to constitute a true collection of art with artistic and heritage strategies. This, in turn, would lead to the involvement of professional players – such as art consultants, insurers, experts and restorers – who would bring solutions to managing artistic heritage.

The Algerian artistic diaspora constitutes a model for young artists and, to a lesser degree, for artists of the same age.

The increasing visibility of artists such as Attia, Tatah, Koraïchi, Benanteur and Ben Bella in museums, galleries and the sales rooms is helping to make young people believe that success is possible for young artists living in Algeria. But they consider that they would have more chance of becoming successful if they settled in Europe. They reproach Algeria's culture ministry for not having created an infrastructure with rules and key players so that there is a full artistic life. The existence of galleries and museums, such as the MAMA, is certainly a necessary condition but mechanisms of public support seem to be missing. There is not a sponsorship law or any assistance for galleries developing the careers of young artists; there are inadequate budgets for museums to acquire artworks; there are not any tax incentives and there are strict, pernickety controls on exporting modern and contemporary artworks. The system is developing solely thanks to the will of art professionals and some collectors. The influence of the diaspora is apparent as a model of success but less so in the artistic content, even though some young artists are sometimes inspired by well-known artists in the diaspora.

Algerian collectors are not numerous; one can count around 20 that have a large collection of over 50 artworks. The collections are centred on Algerian art (Orientalism and/or modern and contemporary art). Historically, collectors have been lawyers and doctors. But today, they are more likely to be industrialists or businessmen that have become wealthy through developing Algeria's private sector in the last 30 years.

These collectors continue to acquire works and are inclined to pay for artworks by Algerian artists at higher prices, providing that the prices correspond to a real quota. This is where Algerian galleries have a role to play. It is no longer enough for them to put on exhibitions or be curators. They must transform themselves into art dealers that are aware of all the market mechanisms and have a due sense of responsibility. A deontology code fixing the rules to observe between artists and galleries, collectors and galleries, and between galleries themselves would be welcome. In the absence of a syndicate of Algerian galleries, the culture ministry could contribute to the market's development by introducing such a code.

Lionel MANGA
Art critic

Pascale Marthine Tayou and Barthélémy Toguo are the two most successful artists originally from Cameroon but living in the diaspora.

Pascale Marthine Tayou

Tayou often comes to Cameroon, where he piloted a project under the umbrella of the Goethe Institute for its fiftieth anniversary. He is a virtuoso of decontextualisation, surpassing everything that resembles a border, be it the borders between nations, the borders separating objects by enclosing them in a space of usage, or those that isolate eras.

Monumental installations constitute Tayou's favourite mode of expression. Whether it's tilting poles hung in a garden or the carcass of a second-hand car brought from Cameroon to Europe, he displaces objects to confer on them hitherto unseen identities that make them eloquent in the exhibition space, by means of mental gymnastics. This exuberant and prolific work, which daringly combines precious crystal with trivial, everyday materials, is deployed within the realm of translation and displacement.

Barthélémy Toguo

Toguo is increasingly present in Bandjoun in the west of Cameroon, where he has built a contemporary art centre called Bandjoun Station. He can be described as a multi-faceted visual artist. From painting, drawing, video and installation to photography, printmaking and performance, Toguo expresses himself across all media in order to treat every aspect of the human condition.

Watercolours in tender colours are never exempt from violence, and nor are his varied compositions, which are sometimes charged with irony and elicit astonishment. Or think of the dolls swathed in bandages in his performance "The Sick Opera" (Palais de Tokyo, 2004), which was rich in uncompromising remarks and political depth. Toguo also enjoys playing with stereotypes. This category-defying aptitude renders him elusive and unpredictable, which is the only trademark of his oeuvre, the expansiveness of which is the never-ending nature of life itself.

The artists of the diaspora don't, strictly speaking, have an impact on the boom and evolution of the local scene, even if one can see in the ever-widening practices, from installation art to performance, a clear effect of the exposure to contemporary art through the media.
However, the pluridisciplinary approach and the fields of questioning that Toguo and Tayou embrace is not yet common among many local artists in Cameroon. Nonetheless, upcoming artists have understood the importance nowadays of imbuing one's practice with theory and having a coherent discourse.
Meanwhile, Simon Njami and Dr. Bonaventure Soh Bejeng Ndikung are the most successful curators with Cameroonian origins. Njami is a recurring guest of the Doual'Art contemporary art centre and recently gave a guest a talk at Galerie MAM in Douala, Cameroon's largest port and main business city. Ndikung founder and artistic director of the art space SAVVY Contemporary in Berlin has been named curator at large of Documenta 14 in Kassel, Germany, and Athens.

NII ANDREWS
Art reviewer

THE EFFECT/INFLUENCE OF THE AFRICAN DIASPORA ON THE GHANAIAN CONTEMPORARY ART MARKET

Understanding the term Diaspora (people settled far from their ancestral homeland) in our current epoch is fraught with many potential problems. The issues become particularly acute when referring to the African Diaspora – a largely global phenomenon.

Our best objective evidence indicates that the ancestral homeland of all humankind is Africa.

Are we then to include almost all of the earth's population located outside the continent? Or should we begin with the Arab slave trade from Africa to the territories of the east that started in 1300?

Surely, an arbitrary set of parameters will enable us to better focus our discussion.

We shall limit the Diaspora to two groups.

First, Ghanaians that have settled (live, work) outside Ghana- and there are an estimated 3-4 million of them.

Up to 200 000 live in the US, the world's largest economy. Only an estimated 5% of them are in the top 10% threshold income level of US$140 000.

Another 80-100 000 live in the UK. The annual remittance contribution (to Ghana) of the US and UK diaspora is US$33 million and US$25 million respectively.

However, two countries in the sub-region; Nigeria and Cote d'Ivoire host 200 000 and 50 000 Ghanaians respectively with annual remittances from Nigeria at US$21 million and the latter at US$12 million.

The proportion of the aforementioned groups earnings spent on Ghanaian contemporary art is not known. It will also be interesting to establish if the amount spent has been increasing over the last decade.

There exists another segment of the African Diaspora with a radically different genesis. It is composed of the descendants of the millions of Africans forcibly extricated from the homeland, taken across, up and down the Atlantic and made to endure the harsh conditions of chattel slavery from 1400-1900.

No, we cannot say that they were immigrants- no matter how well intentioned!

Up till today, they still experience structural long term barriers that make their social integration and upward mobility more difficult than for other groups. There is also among them (as in other Diaspora groups) a group identity that includes the ongoing creation of a community consciousness or mythology which links them to the ancestral land.

Intellectuals, professionals, artists and activists from this group (George Padmore, W.E.B. Dubois, Maya Angelou, Bill Sutherland, Maynard Rustin and others) exerted a not insignificant influence on the thoughts and actions of the mid twentieth century nationalist leaders in Ghana especially Kwame Nkrumah.

Jean Allman describes this as, a time when the West African state of Ghana was a pivotal site for imagining an entirely new, non-aligned world; when Ghanaians, joined by a host of transnational actors (African-American activists and intellectuals, Irish and Welsh nationalists, anti-nuclear peace activists, South African communists, Caribbean Pan-Africanists) cooperated, colluded and collided over how to build a non-racial, anti-imperialist, nuclear free world at the height of the Cold War.

We can surmise that their influence extended to the genesis of the African Personality and the artistic oeuvre of Kofi Antubam, Kobina Bucknor, Saka Acquaye, Vincent Kofi, Amon Kotei, A.O. Bartemius and Oku Ampofo. These artists and others pioneered paradigms in contemporary African art within the liberated cultural space of the newly independent Ghana.

Even when they drew on African traditions in sculpture and iconography, they persevered and formulated alternative artistic ideas thus producing a new art that spoke to the resurgent masses of Ghana. This also resonated with the African Diaspora, particularly in the US, where the Diaspora was then engaged in the epic civil rights struggles of the 50's and 60's.

The power of the African ancestral symbols and aesthetic forms in providing cohesion and focus to African peoples thereby empowering them to confront existential problems cannot be underestimated.

Two examples will suffice.

The Sankofa sign served to encourage African peoples to look to their past in order to retrieve and retain useful indigenous precepts and utilize them for their progress and advancement.

Second, when confronted with the apparent futility of their struggle for emancipation, they could seek to understand that the current setbacks were only temporary; all shall pass except God says the Gye Nyame symbol.

Through the incisive and glamorous interpretation of folk and indigenous African culture, the pioneering Ghanaian contemporary artists provided the ummph for a new social and political dispensation.

Perhaps both groups, on either side of the Atlantic, fed off and nutured each other in ways that were alluded to by the African-American leaders, Martin Luther King and Malcolm X. In the popular culture of that time, it manifested as dashikis, afro combs, nine inch afros and beads… and, "I'm Black and Proud".

Sadly though, within Ghana this indigenous flowering of contemporary art forms has to date not translated into the establishment of a National Museum of Contemporary Art – a commonplace occurrence in the Americas, Europe and Asia.

This lacuna is unacceptable within the context of Ghana's presumed role as a trail blazer in Africa.

But there have been private efforts to collect, promote and showcase Ghanaian contemporary art.

The examples include the Loom, Artists Alliance Gallery, the Dei Foundation and ARTcapital Ghana. These voluntary institutions have permanent displays of superb collections of contemporary Ghanaian artwork and there are always also pieces available for sale.

Specialty exhibitions are also held in these institutions with accompanying well written glossy catalogs thus providing essential documentation on artworks for the local and international market.

The collections include the work of promising young artists and important/established artists who have participated in the ground breaking 1989 "Magiciens de la Terre" show in France, the Venice Biennial, Art Dubai, Art Basle and other important art events frequented by the international jet set, power brokers and trend influencers.

Ghanaian contemporary artists who have benefitted from such international exposure include Ablade Glover, Ato Delaquis, George Afedzi Hughes and Wiz Kudowor.

he huge media publicity generated by such international events for the individual artists is more readily accessible and often much better appreciated by the African Diaspora; much less so for their compatriots domiciled in Ghana.
Consequently, the former are more likely disposed to effect purchases of the artist's work at the "discounted" prices when visiting Ghana.

Needless to state these "discounted" prices are often considered unfavorable by the latter- or perhaps art purchases are very low on their list of priorities.
Another disadvantage for the market is the often unstable nature of the local currency. This works in favor of the diasporan buyer especially when s/he is prepared to buy several pieces.
The hesitancy of the local artists to work solely through gallery owners or a management/marketing team again disadvantages the market. All of these factors make the Ghanaian contemporary art market a buyer's market with peculiar advantages to the diasporan buyer.
Two empirical observations for Ghana are also relevant here.
First, it is much easier for potential patrons to appreciate, relate to and want to purchase artwork when it is viewed in a furnished setting e.g. in a living room or an office instead of the stark white walls of a gallery.
This observation if taken seriously by art dealers should lead to an increase in the number of art buyers.
Second, it is most unusual to find Ghanaian parents visiting an art gallery with their young children. They are much more likely to visit a shopping mall or a fast food joint together. Intuitively this does not auger well for the growth of the future client base for the local art market.

The preponderance of evidence suggests that the economic power of several African states is on the ascendancy in the world just as the US and Europe begins to wane but their cultural power and proclivities remain largely intact.
The overwhelming majority of institutions that dictate the importance and monetary value of art are located in the west.

David Dibosa sums it up as follows, "The big collecting institutions like Tate and Moma operate rather like the big banks. They are always safe, and can guarantee the cultural value of a work of art anywhere, everywhere and forever. Which is why Tate's recognition is such a big deal: it is a stamp of approval that will increase the value and collectability of the work."

However, even though the numbers may be increasing, there are still only a few African diasporans within the power and decision making apparatus of these influential institutions. Clearly, the power dynamic between the loosely structured Ghanaian contemporary art market and the big western collecting institutions is skewed in favor of the latter.

In 2012 when the Guaranty Trust Bank plc, a large Nigerian bank and one of West Africa's most respected partnered Tate in the Tate Africa Program; Tate refused to give figures for its commitment. We could only speculate and hope that the bank's role was substantial.

Finally, the prestige value (or if you like- "cool factor") in owning contemporary african art is not lost on Ghana and Africa's growing list of home grown millionaires and possibly billionaires. Furthermore, this group has shown that it is savvy enough to realize the investment potential in such an asset.
What is interesting is that just ten years ago, the aforementioned factors were only appreciated by a small group of cognoscenti in Ghana and the diaspora. This group is now steadily expanding.
Hopefully, it will not expand to include the significant number of speculators that caused turmoil and overheating in the Western and Asian contemporary art markets.

Only time will tell.

ARTISTS IN THE DIASPORA

- Wanguechi Mutu
- Yinka Shonibare

A PROFILE: Wangechi Mutu
By Osei G. Kofi

> "I was struggling with this idea, that perhaps the reason I was in this situation is I turned into something that didn't belong.
> I didn't belong at home, I didn't belong here. I didn't exist, or I shouldn't exist, in that weird way. Like I'd left and grown on my own like these creatures that grow on Madagascar that are such anomalies. I think there is something about countries and nations that is hard to define. And in fact, that's probably why we create such massive boundaries, because it's so slippery where they begin and where they end. These conservative demarcations of nation and state and culture are soon going to be archaic.
> We have to redefine what we mean when we say "Who are your people?" "Where are you from?""

If you think the 130-odd words cited above and the sentiments therein are from a modern-day philosopher or a social scientist you are wrong. Or, perhaps not so wrong. Eureka – here is world-renowned artist Wangechi Mutu! She was talking to a writer in New York who'd gone to interview the Kenya-born emigree on the eve of her ground-breaking exhibition at the Brooklyn Museum, June 2013.

Wangechi speaks little publicly. But when she does, as in this instance, she bares her soul, poignantly sharing the challenges that assail a nomad who belongs nowhere and everywhere, dealing with constant bifurcation as a fact of life. She's a daughter of Mother Africa, fertilized by the red soils of Kikuyuland, in the shadow of majestic Mount Kenya. Beckoned by goddess Diaspora Wangechi practises her craft far from home. Home, which home? Nairobi where she was born in 1972? America, whose shores she decidedly landed in her search for the golden fleece soon after high school at nuns' run Loreto Convent Msongari, among the best secondary education in Kenya? Her search to hone her natural born talents far from home is paired with a hunger for technical expertise. Subsequently, the studies at the United World College of the Atlantic, Wales. At prestigious Parsons School of Art and Design, New York. At historic Cooper Union for the Advancement of the Arts and Science, New York. Capping it all with a Master's in sculpture from Ivy League Yale, if you please.

Wangechi is arguably the most cerebral and prolific among the dozen plus top-notch diasporic artists wowing museum goers and collectors. Her early art, when she first burst onto the scene, took grotesquerie to a level that would have made Bosch and Arcimboldo blush. She'd scissor images and texts from anthropologic, ethnographic and medical magazines, splicing and spicing them with gems or detritus from high fashion or porn, grafting the lot onto paper and later on mylar, in collages so distinctive they arrested first time viewers in their tracks. In shock and awe. Wangechi's works grab by the throat with their mishmashness, of order in chaos, beauty in horrors, that seem to emerge from our nightmares, or wet dreams, with a surrealist aplomb and Daliesque flair.

Keeping with the spirit of the times Wangechi has segued into sculpture, installation and video, allowing her to better explore her most ardent preoccupations: cultural signifiers and the African identity politics and the atrocities of war, plastic surgery and the body politics, gay and lesbian rights, etc.

The early grotesquerie got Wangechi noticed. Nigerian-born Okwui Enwezor, eminent among the world's power brokers in contemporary art, took her under his wings while she was still in college, including her in the 1997 Johannesburg Biennale which he curated. Enwezor again tapped her to be considered for Deutsche Bank's inaugural Artist of the Year award in 2000 which she won, with a show at their Guggenheim Museum, Berlin.

"Her constant excavation of her process, the constant excavation of her own ideas, and her breaking boundaries within that" are what makes Wangechi so interesting," Enwezor lauded at the award luncheon in New York. Artistic director of the 56th Venice Biennale in 2015, Enwezor gave Wangechi a pride of space in the coveted Giardini where she presented a three-piece showcase: a sculpture of a multi-horned encaged bronze mermaid *She's Got the Whole World*; a collage painting *Forbidden Fruit Picker*; and a video *The End of Carrying It All*, an apocalyptic visual of a Sisyphus figure battling the elements in a vast windblown landscape.

After years of biding time for an interview I finally caught up with the diva around her magistral installation in the Giardini. She was surrounded by a bevy of groupies. The scrum around her was such that all I got was being roped in as an extra in the fashion photo shoot in which she was starring. No time to talk beyond sharing her "admiration and gratitude" for Enwezor. The year before, in 2014, another diasporic mover & shaker Simon Njami of Africa Remix fame included Wangechi in a select group of artists for an artistic enactment of Dante's "The Divine Comedy: Heaven, hell, purgatory revisited by African Contemporary Artists," which Njami curated at the Museum of Modern Art, Frankfurt. In April the stupendously successful show travelled to the National Museum of African Art, Washington DC, for a 4-month run. Wangechi's collage, *The Storm Has Finally Made It Out of Me, Alhamdulillah*, depicting a mystical creature with an explosion emanating from her midsection, was located in hell among other works.

In one of her most recent stunning sculptural works, *Second Dreamer* Wangechi unabashedly took from Brancusi's 1910 Sleeping Muse, which the Romanian-Frenchman had borrowed from Africa's totemic masks. Thus, we now have Africa to Europe to America to Africa! There's also her *Water Woman*, an ebony-black sheen sculpture of Nguva or Mami Water of African folklore, depicted as a nubile with a fetching pair of tits and a lower body of slithery fish, a harking back to the millennia of mermaid mythology also shared by Starbucks' on their coffee cups.

Wangechi has been quoted as using "the aesthetic of rejection and wretchedness to explore the hopeful or sublime." The titles of her works are a world of its own; trenchant, instantly resonant, with deep hidden meanings – never perfunctory, as is the wont of too many among her peers. They surge from the wellspring of her creativity, embodying uplifting pathos, rarely descending into bathos. Sample: *Riding Death in My Sleep*, 2002; *Misguided Little Union, Unforgivable Hierarchies*, 2005; *The Bride Who Married a Camel's Head*, 2009; *The End of eating Everything*, 2013; *Hundred lavish months of bushwhack and Intertwined*, which is one of my favs, showing two scantily clad small-titted damsels with heads of hunting dogs gnawing each other's tongue. Does Wangechi like her women small-titted?

In 17 years since college Wangechi's exhibitions and awards would be the envy of older artists with decades of practice. Someone recently described her art as "like seeing the world through a shaman's eyes." Well, the fact is Wangechi is the shaman. **In 2006-2016 of her 20 solo shows 70% were in museums and public institutions, 30% in private galleries. Of her 155 group shows 86% were in museums and public institutions, 14% in galleries.**

A PROFILE: Yinka Shonibare MBE
By Osei G. Kofi

Art must be fun. It must say something. Which contemporary artist best embodies this uncommon duality? Yinka Shonibare, MBE. He is fun. He is naughty. Never boring. He breaks boundaries. Always evokes something deep. Well, almost always. Huge dollops of humour save Shonibare from humdrum. When the almost entirety of an artist works revolve around fibre glass mannequins and wax prints one must be super talented to always pull it off – and Shonibare does it like a true maestro.

The London-born of Nigerian parents 50-something artist uses his work to explore human foibles, cultural identities, race and class, colonialism, post-colonialism, with their tangled interrelationship between Africa and Europeand the current zeitgeist, Globalisation. Shonibare does it all often with self-deprecation and put-downs that belie the profundity of the subject matters and the messages they carry. While sculpture is his main thing Shonibare has been active in painting, photography, film and performance lately.

A signifier of his art is the brightly coloured wax cotton prints first produced in Indonesia by the Dutch. His trademark media are resin or fibre glass headless mannequins wearing the colourful prints the Dutch exported to West Africa at the beginning of the last century. It caught fashion fire in the hot humid climate. By the 1950s and early independence years the fabric, like the Kente, had become a sign of African pride, notably in Ghana, Cote d'Ivoire, Togo and Benin.

Shonibare makes unique pieces of his sculptural creations. He might make variations of a particular oeuvre, such as the Butterfly Girl and the wind vane series. The latter has had the most international traction lately, with commissions from the US and Germany after it debuted in 2013 in the Yorkshire Sculpture Park. In December 2016 the latest wind vane, Wind Sculpture VII, was erected in front of the Smithsonian's new National Museum of African Art in Washington DC, the first sculpture to be honoured at the prime site.Shonibare was a proponent of installation art way before it became a currency which in the hands of untalented practitioners the genre has turned gimmicky and a real bore.

His first solo exhibition was in 1989 at Byam Shaw Gallery, London. He burst onto the international stage in 2002 with an installation "Gallantry and Criminal Conversation" commissioned by OkwuiEnwezor for Documenta XI in Kassel, a take of humorous bathos on randy Victorians being naughty while pretending they were in serious conversation over serious business.A year later Shonibare gave us Scramble For Africa, 14 life-size mannequins decked out in 19th century costumes of the wax prints around a table somewhere in Europe carving up Africa into exclusive real estates. Measuring 132 x 488 x 280 cm the installation was the Anglo-Nigerian's most evocative memory pitch for Africans. His most iconic work must be How To Blow-Up Two Heads At Once, 2006. Two male mannequins in leather riding boots each with a gun pointed at the other's non-existent head. Difficult to tell who won the duel. There is also a female version.

Talking about epistemic art, Nelson's Ship in a Bottle was Shonibare's most complex and technically challenging work. The medium consisted of a specially blown glass bottle, cork, wood, brass, textiles, acrylic, LED lighting and a ventilation system. At 300 x 535 x 250 cm and a 1:30 scale model of Horatio Nelson's HMS Victory inside, the bottle was moulded by aquarium specialists in Rome. Commissioned by the Greater London Authority for the fourth plinth in Trafalgar Square, the work commemorated the Battle of Trafalgar,the 1805 naval fight by the Royal Navy against the combined fleets of French and Spanish navies in the Napoleonic Wars in which Nelson destroyed 27 Franco-Spanish ships without a single British vessel being lost.

For Shonibare, who describes himself as a "post-colonial" hybrid, the work reflected the relationship between the birth of the British Empire and modern Britain's multi-cultural context. "It's a celebration of London's immense ethnic wealth, giving expression to and honouring the many cultures and ethnicities that are still breathing precious wind into the sails of the United Kingdom," he said. The installation, displayed from May 2010 to January 2012, was so widely admired that at the end of its allotted reign in Trafalgar Square, the UK Art Fund launched a fund raiser to purchase and relocate it at the National Maritime Museum in Greenwich, now its permanent home.

Shonibare's lawyer father moved the family back to Nigeria when the future artist was three. At 17, he returned to Britain for his A-levels at Redrice School, and study fine art, first at Byam School of Art now Central Saint Martin's College, and later at Goldsmiths College where he received his MFA. At 18, Shonibare contracted transverse myelitis, an inflammation of the spinal cord, which resulted in a physical disability that has paralysed one side of his body. He moves about in an electric wheelchair and has assistants making the works under his direction.

In 2004, Shonibare was shortlisted for the Turner Prize. He didn't win but in a BBC website poll 64% of the voters made his work their favourite among the four on the shortlist. Tellingly, he was awarded an MBE that year. An Honorary Doctorate, Fine Artist, from the Royal College of Art followed in 2010. He was elected Royal Academician by the Royal Academy of Arts in 2013. A big deal in the UK.

In 2006-2016 of Shonibare's 45 solo shows 31% were in museums and public institutions, 69% in private galleries. Of his 160 group shows 92% were in museums and public institutions, 8% in galleries.

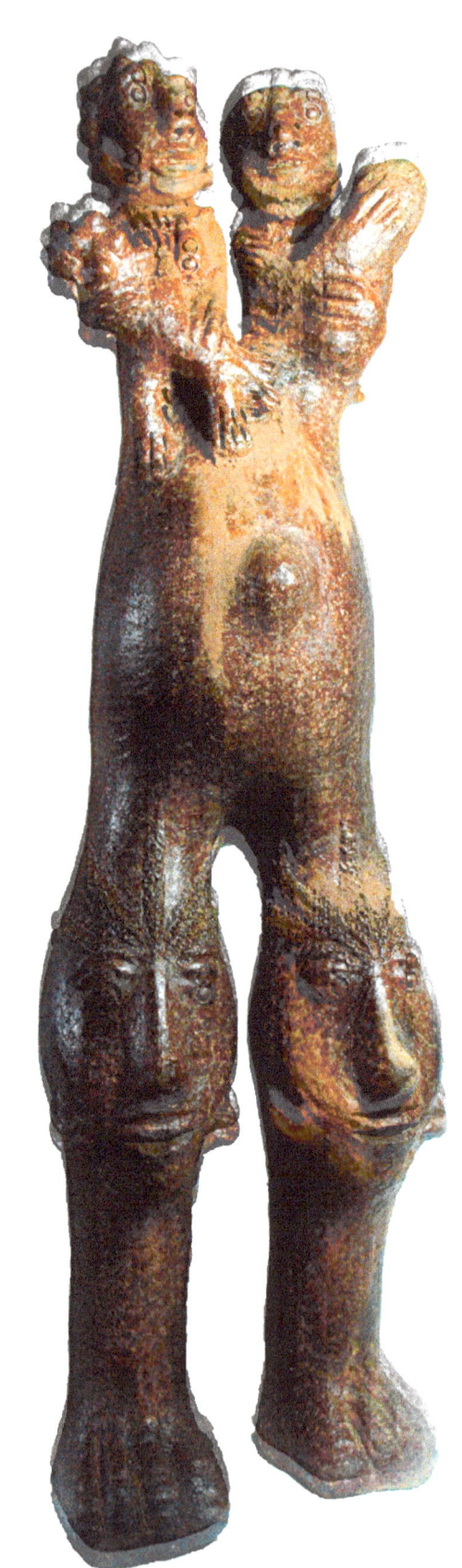

Seyni Awa Camara (b. c. 1945)
Grands genoux, 2008
terracotta
Height 115 cm
court: private collection

2016
TEACH THE FUTURE

- Makgati Molebatsi, art advisor
- Moncef Msakni, owner & director of El Marsa gallery
- Julia Grosse & Yvette Mutumba, co founders of Contemporary And (C&)
- Tumelo Musaka, curator
- Mustapha Orif, art dealer

Makgati Molebatsi
Art advisor

There has been an increase in the interest to acquire art by African Artists, and the market is responding to that. The increase in Art Fairs which focus on art by African artists has contributed to this awareness and visibility. Established fairs which traditionally feature European or Western based galleries have also responded to this visibility by having galleries from Africa featuring as "Guest of honour" or "focus on Africa" for their presence in the fair. Although the FNB Joburg art fair has been in existence for close to ten years - celebrating its tenth year in 2017 - the addition by other art fairs focusing on Contemporary Art by African artists such as 1:54 and Cape Town art fair in the last five years; Artfair X Lagos in Nigeria, Akaa in Paris in 2016 and the inclusion of African galleries in The Armory Show and Art Paris art fair has extended the interest in Art by African artists. Artists whose work is featured in biennales and major exhibition have gained exposure and enhanced the curiosity and desire towards Africa and its artists. The market has responded to this with new galleries opening across the continent, and these galleries showing interest in participating in the art fairs highlighting art by African artists globally.

Moncef Msakni
Owner & director of El Marsa gallery, Tunis

Rediscovering Arab artists as a whole: modern and contemporary.
A remarkable presence of Diaspora artists alike Nadia Kaabi and Ali Tnani.

Julia Grosse & Yvette Mutumba
co-founders of Contemporary And (C&)

What interested us was the events happening on the continent, like the Dakar Biennale in Senegal, which is the oldest biennale in Africa. In 2016, it was a completely international art event with all the collectors and curators from New York attending. Art X, an art fair in Lagos, made its debut last year and was a high-profile, successful first edition. Its founder is Tokini Peterside and its artistic director is Bisi Silva, the founder/artistic director of the Centre for Contemporary Art (CCA), Lagos. Nigeria has a lot of wealthy buyers and a strong collecting scene. Having a professional fair is a good step to bring art to those people, like having Art Basel Hong Kong in Hong Kong. The Also Known As Africa fair, AKAA, also launched its first edition in Paris. It's Europe's second Africa-focused fair after 1:54 in London. I was happy that AKAA could realise its first edition after it had been cancelled the year before, following the terrorist attacks. It makes sense to have this fair in Paris, which has a strong collecting scene interested in African perspectives.

Tumelo Mosaka
Art curator

There were at least three fairs, plus the Dak'Art biennale in Dakar, so there was a real effort to bring art to the public. This was encouraging because we need more art events taking place on the continent in order to educate local audiences so there can be a greater appreciation of artists. Also, several initiatives were launched by artists' collectives to create a platform for dialogue between artists and to show their work to the public.

Mustapha Orif
Art dealer

Two or three exhibitions of young Algerian artists, including an independent group show titled Picturie Générale III featuring 23 artists, highlighted how the level of creativity has bounced back. This was not obvious 10 years ago when the trend for young artists was to "manufacture" copies of Orientalism works in order to satisfy the expectations of the majority of art buyers.

AFRICA ART MARKET TODAY™

**THE CREATIVE ECONOMY
OF THE FASTEST GROWING CONTINENT**

**BESPOKE RESEARCH, ANALYSIS
AND EDUCATION IN THE ART INDUSTRIES**

www.africartmarket.today

Publisher
Africa Art Market™

Editor-in-Chief
Jean Philippe Aka

Deputy Editor
Anna Sansom

Contributors
Osei G. Kofi
Columnist
He's a foreign correspondent and senior editor for a number of media houses including the Reuters News Agency

Mimi Errol
Journalist & art reviewer

Nii Andrews
Art reviewer

Lionel Manga
Art critic

Graphic design
Marjorie Harrold

© 2017 Africa Art Market. All Rights Reserved for all countries. No part of this document may be reproduced or copied in any form or by any means without the written permission from Africa Art Market™. Disclaimer: The information contained herein is general in nature and is not intended as professional advice or opinion provided to the user, nor a recommendation of any particular approach.

www.ingramcontent.com/pod-product-compliance
Lightning Source LLC
Chambersburg PA
CBHW051919210526
45473CB00006B/2070